CLASSIC PAPER TECHNIQUES

FOR GREETING CARDS & GIFTS

INCLUDES QUILLING, STENCILING, WEAVING AND MORE!

CLASSIC PAPER TECHNIQUES

FOR GREETING CARDS & GIFTS

INCLUDES QUILLING, STENCILING, WEAVING AND MORE!

Alisa Harkless

NORTH LIGHT BOOKS
CINCINNATI, OHIO
www.artistsnetwork.com

ABOUT THE AUTHOR

Alisa Harkless is a designer, author and teacher with extensive experience in the
craft industry. She has appeared on the *Carol Duvall Show* and is a regular contributer
to many different craft magazines. Having previously owned her own rubber stamp
store and worked as a sales representative for industry manufacturers, Alisa now works
directly with many companies by helping them design projects for their products. She
has authored *Incredible Ink Techniques* and teaches classes to crafters on a regular basis.
Alisa is married with two children and one dog.

09 08 07 06 05   5 4 3 2 1

Library of Congress Cataloging-in-Publication Data

Harkless, Alisa
  Classis paper techniques for greeting cards & gifts: includes quilling, stenciling, weaving, and
more! / Alisa Harkless.
        p. cm.
  ISBN 1-58180-511-X
  1. Greeting cards. I. Title

TT872.H37 2005
745.594'1--dc22

2004052059

F+W PUBLICATIONS, INC.

Editor: Tonia Davenport
Cover Designer: Marissa Bowers
Interior Designer: Stephanie Strang
Layout Artist: Donna Cozatchy
Production Coordinator: Robin J. Richie
Photographers: Al Parrish, Tim Grondin, Christine Polomsky and Hal Barkan
Photo Stylist: Nora Martini

metric conversion chart

TO CONVERT	TO	MULTIPLY BY
Inches	Centimeters	2.54
Centimeters	Inches	0.4
Feet	Centimeters	30.5
Centimeters	Feet	0.03
Yards	Meters	0.9
Meters	Yards	1.1
Sq. Inches	Sq. Centimeters	6.45
Sq. Centimeters	Sq. Inches	0.16
Sq. Feet	Sq. Meters	0.09
Sq. Meters	Sq. Feet	10.8
Sq. Yards	Sq. Meters	0.8
Sq. Meters	Sq. Yards	1.2
Pounds	Kilograms	0.45
Kilograms	Pounds	2.2
Ounces	Grams	28.4
Grams	Ounces	0.04

ACKNOWLEDGMENTS

I would like to take this opportunity to
thank my family, North Light Books and
the manufacturers in the craft industry
who have been so supportive and generous
in all my creative endeavors.

CONTENTS

» This book is filled with wonderful handmade greeting cards and paper gifts, all made from readily available and simple supplies! You will find that, within this book, the basic supplies stay virtually the same for each and every project. With each chapter a new technique involving paper is explored and some specialized tools are required, and while these tools may be specialized, they will not be hard to find.

Now, let's get to the main ingredient . . . PAPER! Paper is so easy to find in a multitude of colors, textures, styles, types, weights and sizes. Be sure to check out your local craft, rubber stamp, scrapbooking, stationery and fine art stores in your quest for gorgeous paper.

Introduction

This book also emphasizes great embellishment opportunities such as metal charms, rhinestones, ribbon flowers, gold leafing, tassels, wire, metallic thread, ribbon and beads. Hopefully, you will be inspired to keep your eyes open to items that will make unique additions to your projects.

I hope that you will enjoy completing the projects in this book as much as I have enjoyed creating them, and that this will serve as a springboard to creating cards that are as beautiful as they are uniquely your own.

ALISA HARKLESS

BASIC MATERIALS

This section will introduce you to all the basic materials you will need to complete the projects in this book. Some projects will feature specialized materials, but overall, the majority of the projects will utilize the same basic materials over and over again. All these items are readily available and easily found at your local craft, scrapbooking, rubber stamping and art supply stores.

Paper »

Paper is everywhere these days! You don't have to look far to find a huge selection of types, colors and weights. Listed below are only a few of the many different types available.

CARDSTOCK

Cardstock comes in a huge variety of colors and weights. The cardstock that I have used in this book is 80-lb. (216gsm) cardstock. This is an excellent weight for creating your own fold-over cards, for layering techniques and for cutouts.

SCRAPBOOKING PAPER

Scrapbooking paper is generally lightweight and comes in coordinated patterns, prints and solids. The availability of scrapbooking stores and scrapbooking sections in craft stores is endless and offers a large selection of choices.

HANDMADE PAPER

Handmade paper comes in thin, medium and heavy weights. Generally it has a natural look with fibers throughout. Sheet sizes are often large.

VELVET OR SUEDE PAPER

The velvet and suede papers really look like their namesakes. These types of paper add an upscale look and elegant texture to your finished projects.

VELLUM PAPER

Vellum paper is a translucent paper that comes in many color choices as well as printed versions. The use of vellum paper generally adds sophistication to your projects.

METALLIC AND PEARLESCENT PAPER

Metallic and pearlescent papers are offered in lightweight and heavyweight versions, and really put the "wow" in your projects.

CORRUGATED PAPER

Corrugated papers come in many colors and are offered with straight or wavy corrugated lines. You can also create your own corrugated paper with a paper crimper.

JAPANESE WASHI PAPER

Japanese washi papers come in a variety of printed patterns. This elegant paper adds a touch of Asian flair to your projects and is a popular choice for origami and tea bag folding.

Adhesives »

The adhesives that I use most frequently are double-stick tape, glue stick, ⅛" (3mm) thick foam tape and craft glue. These are described further in the Basic Techniques section on page 13 and there are pros and cons to each.

Some other great adhesive options you may wish to have on hand are listed below along with brief descriptions of their use.

DRAFTING TAPE

Drafting tape holds things in place temporarily.

GLUE DOTS

Glue dots are great for applying bows, ribbon flowers, buttons, and so on. They are not well-suited for heavier items.

VELLUM TAPE

Vellum tape is used with vellum paper and is less likely to show through the paper than other tapes.

GLASS, METAL AND PLASTIC ADHESIVE

Glue made for glass, metal and plastic is superstrong and will adhere to nonporous items very well. It does take a bit of time to cure completely.

Cutting Tools »

My favorite cutting tools include the paper cutter, craft knife and decorative paper punches. Each of these is discussed further in the Basic Techniques section on page 12.

In addition to regular scissors, I enjoy using all types of decorative-edged scissors. My favorite type of decorative scissors creates a deckle-edged cut. I like this cut because there is no need to realign a specific pattern each time I make a new cut. This allows me to speed along in my creative endeavors.

A couple of other cutting tools will be used for the projects in this book, and you may want to consider these, as well.

STANDARD HOLE PUNCHES

The following sizes are the most common hole punches and are good to have around: $\frac{1}{16}$", $\frac{1}{8}$" and $\frac{1}{4}$" (2mm, 3mm and 6mm). Not only will a collection of these sizes satisfy your needs, but these are the standard available sizes for eyelets also.

JAPANESE SCREW PUNCH

A wonderful hole punch option, the Japanese screw punch allows you to easily make a hole where a handheld punch might not reach.

Other Tools »

There are a few more tools that can help you bring sophistication to your papercrafts, and once you give them a try, you may even find more creative uses for them than the ones mentioned in this book.

STYLUS

I use a stylus for scoring paper, but a bone folder works equally well. The stylus is also used to dry emboss, but we will discuss that in more detail in the Dry Embossing section (see page 28).

BRAYER

While a brayer is normally used to apply ink, I find it works great to smooth layers of paper that are glued together. It really helps get all the air bubbles out.

EYELET SETTING TOOL AND HAMMER

I love using eyelets, and the techniques for setting them are covered in the next section. To use eyelets as an embellishment in your projects, you will need an eyelet setting tool, a hammer and a protective surface.

Embellishments »

Always be on the lookout for great embellishment opportunities. It is fun to add unique items to a finished project. Listed below are some of my ideas for embellishment:

- Metal charms
- Tassels
- Mizuhiki cord
- Rhinestones
- Wire
- Ribbon roses and flowers
- Assorted wired ribbon and satin ribbon
- Eyelets
- Raffia

- Decorative threads
- Glass beads
- Flat-backed marbles
- Small seashells
- Buttons
- Yarn and fibers
- Shipping tags
- Colored sand
- Stickers and die-cuts

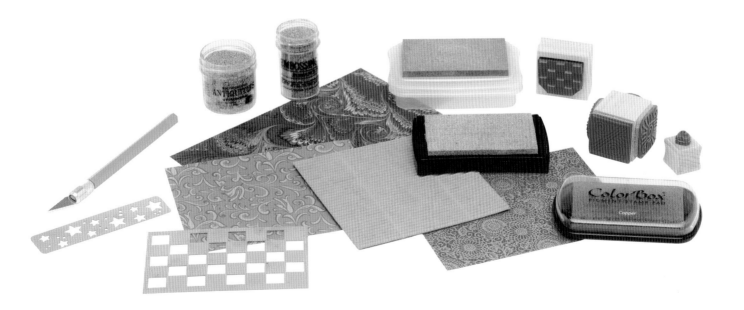

BASIC
TECHNIQUES

The basic techniques listed in this section are utilized time and time again throughout the book. Familiarize yourself with this section so that you will be able to easily complete all the projects. Specialized techniques, specific to a particular project, are explained within each chapter in a step-by-step fashion.

Using Tools to Cut Paper »

Several tools are available to trim the paper you will need for your papercrafts. The ones listed here are the ones that I've found make cutting the easiest.

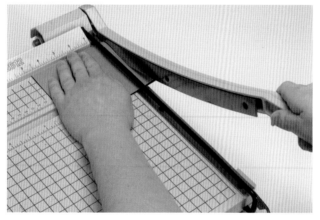

TRIMMING WITH A PAPER CUTTER | A paper cutter provides accurate and nice, straight cuts. Be sure your paper is aligned squarely with the guide at the top and that it is at the desired measurement. A paper cutter is my favorite tool for cutting paper because it's the fastest.

TRIMMING WITH A CRAFT KNIFE | For straight cuts, place the paper on a cutting mat and a metal ruler face down on the paper, so that the cork side is up. Hold the ruler securely with one hand as you drag the craft knife down along the edge of the ruler. Be sure your fingers are out of the way! Align the paper and the ruler with the lines on the mat's grid to make 90° cuts.

USING A DECORATIVE PAPER PUNCH | Using a punch while you are standing will give you more leverage. A dull blade can be sharpened by punching through waxed paper, followed by tin foil. Turning the punch upside down allows you to see more easily where you are punching, if placement is important.

USING A JAPANESE SCREW PUNCH | A Japanese screw punch is a great tool that comes with interchangeable tips. It is able to punch through many layers at a time, in any location on the surface. Simply press down into the paper while gripping the handle and then release.

Using Adhesives for Paper ≫

Using the proper adhesive for the right application can affect the finished quality of your papercrafts.

ADHERING WITH DOUBLE-STICK TAPE | Double-stick tape is good to use for vellum or heavier-weight paper with straight cuts. Line all paper edges with the tape to prevent future lifting. One advantage to this type of adhesive is that it will not warp or weaken the paper.

GLUING OVER A SOLID AREA | Glue stick is good for lighter-weight papers or those with irregular or intricate edges. Complete coverage is important to prevent bubbles. Scrap paper under the glued surface allows you to run the stick off the edge of the paper.

GLUING OVER CUTOUT AREAS | For pieces of paper that have cut-out areas, place a piece of scrap paper under the surface to be glued. Use the glue stick in a dabbing, rather than running, motion to prevent the glue from seeping under the open areas.

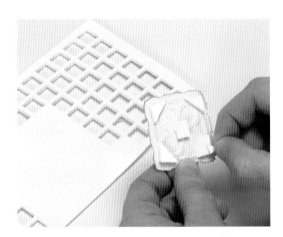

CREATING DEPTH FOR ELEMENTS | Foam tape both adheres papers together and adds depth to a project. For the projects in this book, ⅛" (3mm) thick tape will work the best. Punch out one square and snip it down into smaller pieces to distribute evenly underneath the image to be layered. Remember to include a piece in the center of the image to prevent sagging.

USING CRAFT GLUE FOR EMBELLISHMENTS | Use craft glue to adhere charms and other embellishments. When adhering charms, the hollowed-out area will need to be filled with glue to make contact with the paper. Clear-drying glue will be the most forgiving. It is also a good glue for adhering heavy papers such as a paper casting (see page 81).

Eyelet Setting »

Adding eyelets to your projects is an easy way to secure two or more pieces of paper together and add an attractive embellishment all in one! Eyelets are available in many sizes, shapes and colors.

one »

PUNCH A HOLE | Using a hole punch that is the same size as the eyelet you are using, make a hole in the paper. The size used for projects in this book is ⅛" (3mm).

two »

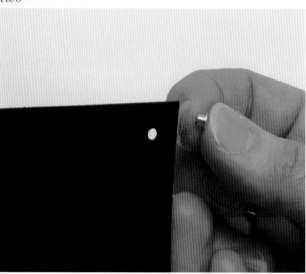

INSERT THE EYELET | Insert one eyelet through the front of the paper piece.

three »

TURN OVER AND SET | Turn the paper piece over onto a protective surface such as a piece of wood. Place the eyelet setting tool on the top of the eyelet's shank and lightly hammer down to spread the shank apart.

four »

VIEW FINISHED PIECE | Turn the piece back over and view from the front.

Scoring to Make a Folded Card »

Many colors of cardstock are sold in packages as prefolded cards, but if you are like me, you don't want to limit yourself to standard sizes or a smaller choice of color. Creating your own folded cards from a larger piece of cardstock is easy. Cut down a piece of paper that is the height and twice the width of the desired finished card size. Sometimes a square shape is a nice change.

one »

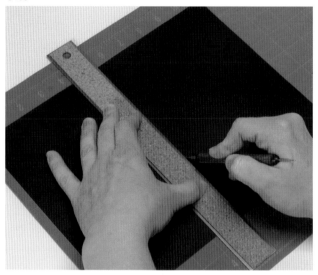

LINE UP PAPER AND RULER | Using the cutting mat as a guide, align the top edge of the paper with a horizontal line on the grid. At the center point of the paper, align the ruler with a vertical line on the grid. Using either a bone folder or a stylus, apply a line of pressure to the card down the length of the ruler.

two »

REMOVE RULER AND REVEAL SCORED LINE | There should now be a shiny line down the center of the card. This is where you will fold it.

three »

FOLD THE PAPER | Fold the paper on the line and crease flat with a bone folder.

In recent years, the art of rubber stamping has really evolved from that of craft to fine art. Stamped images are great for freeing up the creative juices of those who are less likely to enjoy illustrating or drawing but love working with color, texture and design. Staring at a blank piece of cardstock no longer has to leave an artist stymied. The image from a chosen stamp alone is often just what you need to get things rolling.

In this section you will learn how to use rubber stamps to create really attractive and quite unique greeting cards. Rubber stamps are readily available in your local craft and specialty stores. You can try so many interesting and endless applications. Assorted images, inks, embossing powders, embellishments and techniques make for a never-ending supply of possibilities. Give these unique projects a try for yourself or make them for someone you love!

Rubber Stamping

DIMENSIONAL ROSE CARD

GILDED CARD

STAMPING
B A S I C S

Materials

Before creating stamped art of your own, it's good to familiarize yourself with the basic tools and materials needed. Experimenting with different images, inks and powders is the only way to learn what works best for you, so don't be intimidated about going in a new direction. Once you start stamping, it's hard to stop!

RUBBER STAMPS

Rubber stamps are easily found in your local craft stores as well as specialty rubber stamp, scrapbooking and paper stores. Each rubber stamp can be used for a variety of techniques and projects.

INK PADS

A huge variety of types and colors of ink pads is available. Not all ink pads are the same. Certain techniques require ink pads with specific properties. Read the label of the ink pad carefully to find the type you will need for your specific project.

HEAT GUN

A heat gun is primarily used to melt embossing powder that is used with rubber stamps and either embossing ink or a pigment-based ink. While many rubber stamp projects do not require the use of embossing powder and a

heat gun, it is good to have one on hand to heat-set various inks and to speed drying time.

OTHER ITEMS TO HAVE ON HAND

EMBOSSING POWDERS are made from a resin that melts when heat is applied with a heat gun, thus creating an embossed or raised surface. Embossing powder works best when applied over a slow-drying ink called pigment ink. Several types of these powders are described below.

CLEAR EMBOSSING POWDER appears white in the jar but melts clear. It is often applied over an image that has been stamped with a colored pigment ink to create a high-gloss effect.

COLORED EMBOSSING POWDER comes in a large variety of colors. Sometimes several different colors of embossing powder are mixed together in one jar to achieve an interesting multicolor effect.

DETAIL EMBOSSING POWDER is ground finely and works wonderfully with very detailed rubber-stamped images.

ULTRATHICK EMBOSSING POWDER lets you achieve thick and bold images. It comes in clear as well as a variety of colors and works best with bold-lined images.

TACKY EMBOSSING POWDER becomes a glue when heated, so you can apply glitter, gold leaf, mica powder, or other fine-grained substances to the rubber-stamped image. It should be worked with quickly, however, because as the melted powder cools, it becomes less sticky.

Techniques

To begin creating works of art with rubber stamps, keep in mind just a few simple techniques. You will find that different papers react to ink differently, and detailed images may work for you better on surfaces that are less porous, like glossy cardstock. Trial and error is really the key. With so many beautiful images and such a selection of inks and powders, you won't run out of ideas anytime soon!

one »

INK THE STAMP | To apply an even layer of ink to a stamp, lay the stamp image-side-up on a firm surface. Tap ink onto the stamp with a raised ink pad, being sure to cover the entire image area with ink. It is all right to go over an area more than once.

two »

STAMP THE IMAGE | With the paper to be stamped on a firm surface, press the stamp down firmly and do not rock or shift the stamp. Lift the stamp straight up.

three »

Tip! **Since vellum paper has a tendency to curl when heated, be sure to preheat your heat gun before applying heat to the vellum paper. This will ensure that you will melt the embossing powder quickly with an already hot heat gun and the vellum paper will be less likely to curl.**

ADD EMBOSSING POWDER, IF DESIRED | If you have stamped with a pigment or slow-drying ink, you can sprinkle embossing powder onto the stamped image. Tap off the excess onto a scrap piece of paper and return it to its container. Heat the powdered image with a heat gun to melt the powder and give the image a raised look. Embossing powders come in many colors and textures, including clear and metallics. Some can even create a rusted or patina texture to enhance your image.

dimensional ROSE CARD

This greeting card project will teach you how to create a three-dimensional rose using paper, rubber stamps and adhesive-backed foam dots. Once learned, this technique will cause you to look at your rubber stamp collection in a whole new way! This card would work well for a wedding, an anniversary or a special lady's birthday.

materials

- dark green cardstock (2 sheets)
- gold cardstock
- mauve cardstock
- light green cardstock
- white pearlescent paper (3 sheets)
- Memories Barn Red ink pad (Stewart Superior)
- Memories Hunter Green ink pad (Stewart Superior)
- butterfly charm
- gold and cream tassel

- double-stick tape
- ⅛" (3mm) adhesive foam dots
- glue stick
- brayer
- floral border punch
- scissors
- ⅛" (3mm) hole punch
- rose stamp (Stampendous)
- leaf trio stamp (Stampendous)

PAPER PREPARATION ≫

Trim the following papers to the given sizes:

dark green cardstock: 10" x 7" (25.4cm x 17.8cm) folded to 5" x 7" (12.7cm x 17.8cm), 4½" x 4⅞" (11.4cm x 12.4cm), 3¾" x 5½" (9.5cm x 14cm), 2¾" x 5½" (7cm x 14cm), 1¾" x 5½" (4.5cm x 14cm)

gold cardstock: 4¾" x 5⅛" (12cm x 13cm)

mauve cardstock: 7" x 6½" (17.8cm x 16.5cm)

light green cardstock: 4¼"x 5½" (10.8cm x 14cm)

white pearlescent paper (3 sheets): 4" x 5½" (10.2cm x 14cm), 4" x 4⅜" (10.2cm x 11cm), 3" x 5½" (7.6cm x 14cm), 2" x 5½" (5cm x 14cm)

one »

LAYER BASE PIECES OF CARDSTOCK | Adhere gold cardstock, 4½" x 4⅞" (11.4cm x 12.4cm) dark green cardstock and 4" x 4⅜" (10.2cm x 11.1cm) white pearlescent paper onto the folded green cardstock. Attach all of the layers with double-stick tape around all four sides. Smooth down all the layers with a brayer.

two »

PUNCH PEARLESCENT PAPER | Using the floral border punch, punch the long edges of the remaining white pearlescent paper pieces. Make the first punch, then line up the subsequent punches using the guides printed on the punch.

three »

PUNCH OPPOSITE SIDES | For the second sides, turn the papers over and begin at the same edge as the first side so that the pattern will match along both sides.

four »

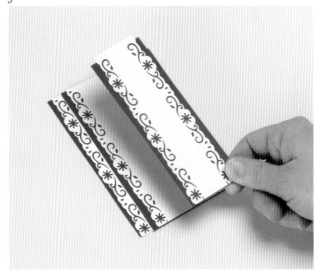

TRIM OFF EXCESS PAPER AND LAYER | Trim off any attached excess border with scissors. Attach each of the three pearlescent pieces to the remaining three pieces of dark green cardstock, using double-stick tape. Layer these three pieces, largest to smallest. Align the punched flower pattern as each piece is adhered.

five »

LAYER PUNCHED PIECES ONTO THE CARDS | Trim the uneven heights along the top and bottom to a total length of 4⅛" (10.5cm). Adhere this finished piece to the white pearlescent paper on the card with double-stick tape. Brayer down all pieces to secure.

six »

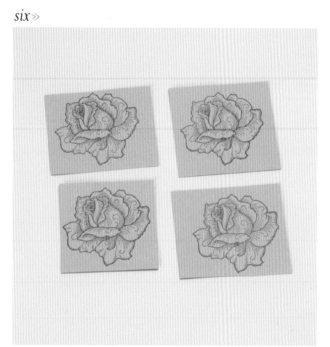

seven »

STAMP THE ROSES | Stamp four roses onto the mauve cardstock with the Barn Red ink. Cut these four pieces apart to make each one easier to work with.

CUT OUT THE ROSE SECTIONS | Beginning with one rose, take scissors and cut out the entire rose. Cut out all but one petal on the second rose; then for the third and fourth roses, make two different, progressively smaller sizes, as shown.

STAMP THE LEAVES | Stamp two leaf groups onto the light green cardstock, using the Hunter Green ink. Cut one leaf group out in its entirety and cut out just the leaves of the second group, as shown.

LAYER THE ROSE | Begin with the largest rose piece on the table. Apply three or four small foam dots over the back of the next largest piece and attach that to the rose on the table. Continue layering the third and fourth rose pieces with the foam dots. For the smaller sections, cut down foam dots to small pieces as needed.

ten

ASSEMBLE PIECES ONTO THE CARD | Attach all leaf pieces to the bottom of the card, using a glue stick (refer to photo for placement). Carefully apply glue stick to the back of the rose and adhere it overlapping the leaf pieces. Adhere three or four foam dots to the back of the butterfly charm and position it in the upper right corner of the card.

eleven

ADD TASSEL TO FINISH | With the ⅛" (3mm) hole punch, make two holes, ¼" (6mm) apart, one on top of the other, in the upper left corner of the card. Fold the tassel in half and thread the folded portion through the bottom hole first, and then bring the folded portion up through the top hole. Tie a knot with each of the long ends.

gilded CARD

This project will teach you how to stamp and emboss with a tacky embossing powder that will enable you to adhere gold leaf flakes to the stamped image. Bold, wide-lined images are your best choice for this type of technique. The masculine style of this card makes it great for the man in your life. It is also well suited as an upscale party invitation.

materials

- black cardstock (2 sheets)
- copper paper
- clear embossing ink pad
- Encore Ultimate Metallic Bronze ink pad (Tsukineko)
- tacky embossing powder
- gold leafing flakes
- gold Mizuhiki cord, 36" (91cm) cut to four equal pieces
- glue stick
- double-stick tape
- ⅛" (3mm) adhesive foam dots
- masking tape
- clear-drying craft glue
- heat gun
- dry sponge
- deckle-edged scissors
- scissors
- scrap paper
- brayer
- dragonfly punch
- Aztec border rubber stamp (Inkadinkado)

PAPER PREPARATION

Trim the following papers to the given sizes:

black cardstock: 11" x 5½" (28cm x 14cm) folded to 5½" x 5½" (14cm x 14cm), 8½" x 11" (21.6cm x 28cm), 5" x 5" (12.7cm x 12.7cm), 1¾" x 1¾" (4.5cm x 4.5cm)

copper paper: 5¼" x 5¼" (13.3cm x 13.3cm), 1¾" x 1¾" (4.5cm x 4.5cm), 1½" x 1½" (3.8cm x 3.8cm)

one »

INK THE BORDER STAMP | Ink the Aztec border stamp with clear embossing ink and stamp onto the narrow width of the 8½" x 11" (21.6cm x 28cm) black cardstock. Sprinkle with tacky embossing powder, tap off excess onto the scrap paper and heat with the heat gun. The powder will melt clear but remain tacky.

two »

ADD GOLD LEAFING FLAKES | Sprinkle flakes of gold leafing onto the embossed image.

three »

WIPE OFF EXCESS | Gently wipe away excess leafing and put the excess back in the original container. With a dry sponge, rub the image to remove remaining leafing from cracks and crevices and to expose the stamped image. Stamp, emboss and gold leaf three more strips in this same manner.

four »

CUT OUT THE STRIPS | Cut out each strip with the deckle-edged scissors, leaving an edge that measures approximately ⅛" (3mm) on either side of the image.

five »

GILD THE STRIP EDGES | Hold one of the strips tightly in your fingers and tap the deckled edges onto the bronze ink pad to add a little color and definition to the edges. Repeat for both sides of each of the four strips. Place strips on a piece of scrap paper to dry, or you can heat-set them with the heat gun.

Tip ! **When working with embossing powders, or any fine-particled embellishment, shake the excess off into a coffee filter for a quick means of refunneling the product back into its original container.**

TRIM AND LAYER THE STRIPS | When the strips are dry, cut each of them to measure 5" (12.7cm). Save the excess trimmed edges to use on another project. Apply glue stick to the back of one strip and place it on one edge of the 5" x 5" (12.7cm x 12.7cm) black cardstock, leaving the left edge slightly loose. Place the second strip overlapping the first, and the third strip overlapping the second. Place the fourth strip down and tuck it under the left side of the first strip. Leave an equal border along each strip.

seven

LAYER ONTO THE CARD | Adhere the large piece of copper paper to the black fold-over card with double-stick tape. Brayer to secure. Use double-stick tape to attach the woven piece to the layered card. Apply glue stick to the piece of copper paper measuring 1¾" x 1¾" (4.5cm x 4.5cm) and place it in the center of the woven strips. Use your brayer to secure the pieces in place.

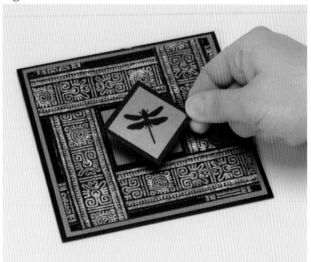

ADD THE DRAGONFLY | Use a glue stick to adhere the last piece of copper paper to the black cardstock square measuring 1¾" x 1¾" (4.5cm x 4.5cm). Punch a dragonfly out of excess black cardstock. Adhere the dragonfly with glue stick and attach it to the copper paper on the diagonal. Cut two adhesive foam dots on the diagonal and place an adhesive-backed foam triangle in each corner of the back of the black piece. Remove the backing and place the layered piece on the diagonal in the center of the card.

TRIM THE GOLD CORD | Cut the Mizuhiki cord into four 9" (23cm) lengths. Run your fingernail down each piece of cord to get it to start curling and to loosen it up a bit.

ten »

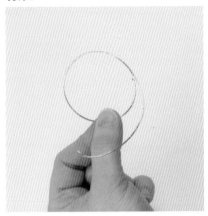

BEGIN THE FIRST LOOP │ Hold the cord in your left hand (for right-handed people; right for left-handed people) at about 1" (2.5cm) from the end of the cord.

eleven »

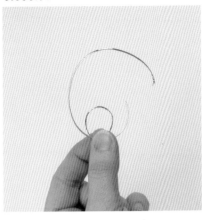

SECURE IN ONE HAND │ Make a loop with the Mizuhiki cord and pinch with the fingers of your left hand to hold it in place.

twelve »

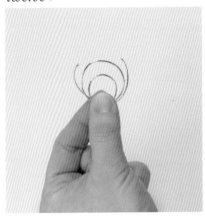

BEGIN THE SECOND LOOP │ Make a second larger loop with the rest of the Mizuhiki cord and again pinch with the fingers of your left hand to hold it in place.

thirteen »

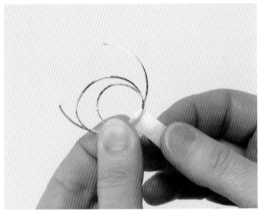

SECURE THE LOOPS WITH TAPE │ Adjust the loops and tails, then secure the Mizuhiki cord (where you've been holding it) with a small piece of masking tape. Repeat for each of the four pieces of Mizuhiki cord.

fourteen »

ADD LOOPS TO THE CARD TO FINISH │ Apply a small amount of clear-drying craft glue under one side of the raised cardstock square. Place one of the Mizuhiki cord loops into the glue where the masking tape is located. Use scissors or another narrow tool to push the Mizuhiki cord loops under the cardstock and into the glue. Repeat for the other three Mizuhiki cord loops. Set aside to dry.

Texture makes things more interesting, and an embossed image gives depth and elegance to your papercrafts. Dry embossing is simply creating an image on paper or vellum that is raised from the surface and tangible. A brass stencil is the most common tool used to provide an embossed image, and these stencils are available in numerous sizes and styles to fit any occasion. Stencils come both with and without text. The ones that are text-free can be flipped to give you a mirror image if desired, creating even more possibilities. In addition, you may choose to use only part of the stencil in your design, or repeat another portion in a different spot on the same project.

In this chapter I would like to introduce you to the basics of dry embossing. The tools needed for dry embossing are basic—a metal embossing template, a lightbox, a stylus and paper. The approach described in this section will give your paper creations a subtle, yet sophisticated look.

Dry Embossing

BLACK METALLIC CARD

THREE HEARTS CARD

FAUX PARCHMENT CARD

EMBOSSING
B A S I C S

Materials

The tools and materials you will need to try a hand at dry embossing are minimal. Paper, a brass template, a stylus and a lightbox are really all you need. Experiment with different colors and weights of paper. Typically, dark-colored papers are not transparent enough to see through with the lightbox, but that will depend on your particular box and the exact weight of the paper. When in doubt, watercolor paper, vellum and light-colored cardstock are almost always safe bets.

METAL EMBOSSING TEMPLATES
Metal embossing templates are used to dry emboss paper. An image is created from the open areas of the template. Many shapes, sizes and styles are available. These templates may also be used to stencil color onto a flat surface.

STYLUS
A stylus is a two-sided tool that has a round metal ball on each end, one slightly larger than the other. Styli come in two standard sizes, and having both would provide a total of four different-sized metal balls for dry embossing. The majority of the time you will use the largest-size ball, but having all of the sizes available to you can really come in handy.

LIGHTBOX
A lightbox will enable you to see through most light-colored papers and some dark-colored papers. For

dark paper, test each type by laying it on a lit lightbox with a stencil underneath. If you do not have access to a lightbox, a sunny window can fill in as an alternative.

DRAFTING TAPE
Drafting tape is a low-tack tape used to help hold your metal stencil in place while dry embossing.

WAXED PAPER
Rubbing waxed paper over the surface to be dry embossed will help slicken the paper surface, making it much easier for the stylus to glide across the paper.

Techniques

The single most important thing to remember when dry embossing is the orientation of your stencil. Be certain it is facing the way you want it to when taping it to your paper!

one »

POSITION THE METAL EMBOSSING TEMPLATE | Position the metal embossing template on the front side of your paper the way you would like it to appear. This is especially important for a template that includes words. Secure the template in place with drafting tape.

two »

TURN THE PAPER AND TEMPLATE OVER | Turn the template face down and rub waxed paper over the surface of the paper that is to be embossed. Place the paper and template on the lightbox (template side down). The light from the lightbox will allow you to see through the paper and visualize each opening of the metal embossing template. Using the stylus, apply pressure and trace along the lines of all openings of the template. Take care to follow and include all parts of the template. Use the smaller-size balls of the stylus as needed for smaller openings and more defined areas.

three »

REMOVE TEMPLATE |
When all areas have been embossed, turn the paper back over and gently remove the tape and template from the paper.

Tip! **Be sure not to dry emboss over taped areas. Sometimes this burnishes the tape to the paper. When the tape is removed, it might pull up the top layer of the paper. If necessary, remove and replace each piece of tape as you come to it.**

black metallic CARD

With this project highlighting dry embossing, I was actually able to find a dark paper that I could see through on the lightbox. The black paper is textured and glossy, which only adds to the unusual metallic effect of this card! Additional metallic paper layers, metallic inks, a tassel and metal photo corners further enhance this eye-catching card.

materials

- black cardstock
- brushed metal black cardstock
- copper cardstock
- Brilliance Platinum Planet ink pad (Tsukineko)
- Brilliance Galaxy Gold ink pad (Tsukineko)
- Brilliance Cosmic Copper ink pad (Tsukineko)
- gold and black tassel
- metal photo corners (4)
- drafting tape
- three cosmetic sponge wedges
- double-stick tape
- clear-drying craft glue
- waxed paper
- lightbox
- stylus
- scissors
- photo corner edger scissors
- circular stained glass metal embossing template

PAPER PREPARATION ≫

Trim the following papers to the given sizes:

black cardstock: 11" x 5½" (28cm x 14cm) folded to 5½" x 5½" (14cm x 14cm)

brushed metal black cardstock: 5½" x 5½" (14cm x 14cm), 4¾" x 4¾" (12.1cm x 12.1cm)

copper cardstock: 4½" x 4½" (11.4cm x 11.4cm)

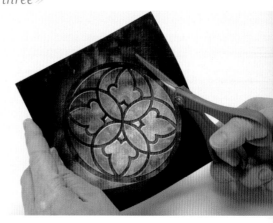

ADD COLOR TO EMBOSSING |
Create an embossed image onto the brushed metal black cardstock (see Techniques, page 31). Include the outside of the circle when you're embossing. Turn the paper back over and leave the metal embossing template in place. Tear a portion off of the bottom of each cosmetic wedge to prevent a "square" image as the color is applied. Firmly dab the sponge into the silver inkpad to ink it up. Dab ink onto the center area of the metal embossing template. Continue in a circular motion dabbing color to form about a 1½" (3.8cm) diameter of ink.

CONTINUE ADDING COLOR | Then dab the gold ink around the silver ink, overlapping slightly to form about a 2¾" (7cm) diameter of ink. Lastly, dab the copper ink around the outer perimeter of the circle. Don't worry if color goes outside of the stencil.

REMOVE TEMPLATE AND TRIM |
Carefully remove the metal embossing template and wipe the excess ink off of the template. Allow the ink to dry for several minutes on the paper. Cut out the circle with scissors, using the outside embossed line as a guide.

five »

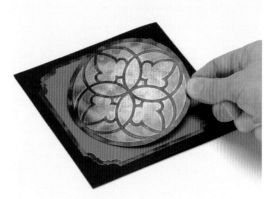

LAYER ON COPPER PAPER |
Using double-stick tape, adhere the brushed metal black cardstock to the black card. Then layer the copper cardstock and finally the embossed and inked circle. Carefully center each layer.

four »

six »

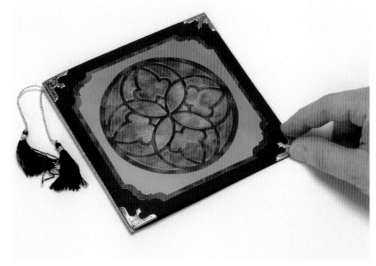

CREATE DECORATIVE CORNERS | Cut each corner of the copper cardstock with the photo corner edgers. Insert the corner of the cardstock into the convex side of the scissors as far as it will go and then cut. Cut out all four corners and then repeat with the remaining piece of brushed metal black cardstock.

ADD TASSEL AND METAL CORNERS | Drape the tassel through the fold of the card and tie at the top. Lastly, glue the four photo corners to the outside edges of the black card using clear-drying craft glue. Set aside to dry.

three hearts CARD

Dry embossing can be done on translucent vellum paper without the use of a lightbox. The dry-embossed areas on either white or colored vellum will turn white. This makes the vellum appear lacy. In this project we will also use a small hole punch to make the three hearts look even more lacelike. This style is great for weddings, baby showers or any elegant occasion!

materials

- white cardstock
- silver cardstock
- white or transluscent vellum
- pink velveteen paper
- pink ribbon flowers (3)
- drafting tape
- double-stick tape
- craft-size Glue Dots
- waxed paper
- stylus
- scissors
- 1/16" (2mm) hole punch
- decorative corner edgers
- eyelet lace heart metal embossing template

PAPER PREPARATION »

Trim the following papers to the given sizes:

white cardstock: 10" x 7" (25.4cm x 17.8cm) folded to 5" x 7" (12.7cm x 17.8cm)

silver cardstock: 4½" x 6½" (11.4cm x 16.5cm)

white or transluscent vellum: 4" x 4¼" (10.2cm x 10.8cm) (3 total)

pink velveteen paper: 4¼" x 6¼" (10.8cm x 16cm)

one »

EMBOSS HEART | Adhere the heart stencil onto a piece of vellum with drafting tape. Turn the vellum over and rub the piece with waxed paper. Using the larger stylus, trace all areas of the stencil, including the dots and the inside line of the heart.

two »

PUNCH OUT DOTS | Remove the tape and the stencil. Using scissors, cut out the heart, following the scalloped lines. Use a ¹⁄₁₆" (2mm) hole punch to punch out all the small white dots. Repeat both steps to make two more hearts.

three »

CUT CORNERS AND LAYER CARD | Using the decorative corner edgers, cut all four corners of the pink velveteen paper. Repeat with the silver cardstock and with the folded white card. For the folded white card, you can cut through two layers at the same time. Use double-stick tape to adhere the silver paper and pink velveteen paper onto the white card.

Tip! **Although subtle, double-stick tape is not completely invisible under vellum. When using double-stick tape, be sure to strategically place each piece where it will be less likely to be seen. A tape specifically made for adhering vellum is available in your local craft stores.**

four »

ADHERE HEARTS TO CARD | Take a small piece of double-stick tape and place it near the top of one of the hearts (underneath where a pink ribbon flower will be placed). Place this near the top of the card on the pink velveteen paper. Repeat with the middle and then the bottom heart, spacing each heart out evenly.

five »

ADD RIBBONS | Attach a pink ribbon flower, using craft-size Glue Dots, to the top of each heart.

faux parchment CARD

In this project you will combine both rubber–stamping and dry–embossing techniques to fashion a card with a faux parchment appearance. A Pergamano embossing pad is a special pad used in parchment craft instead of a lightbox and metal template. This card speeds up the process by stamping and embossing the background and the dragonfly images, then dry embossing select areas of the dragonfly to create dimension and turn the vellum paper white. This is a simple process that creates unbelievable results!

materials

- peach cardstock
- white vellum paper
- white pigment ink pad
- white embossing powder
- coral brush marker
- 4" (102mm) 20-gauge silver wire
- small rhinestones
- vellum tape
- jar wax (Perga Soft)
- clear-drying craft glue
- heat gun
- scissors
- paper cutter
- Pergamano embossing pad
- stylus
- round-nose pliers
- scrap paper
- toothpicks
- small cup of water
- Battenburg background rubber stamp
- Battenburg dragonfly rubber stamp

PAPER PREPARATION »

Trim the following papers to the given sizes:

peach cardstock: 8½" x 5½" (21.6cm x 14cm) folded to 4¼" x 5½" (10.8cm x 14cm)

white vellum paper: 5½" x 8½" (14cm x 21.6cm), 4¼" x 5½" (10.8cm x 14cm)

one »

EMBOSS LACE BACKGROUND | Ink the background stamp with white pigment ink. Stamp the image on the bottom half of the large piece of vellum, with the wavy design at the bottom of the sheet. Sprinkle white embossing powder onto the image and tap off the excess. (Refer to the rubber stamping chapter, beginning on page 16, for further embossing information.) Heat the embossing powder with the heat gun to melt the powder.

two »

FOLD AND TRIM VELLUM | Fold the vellum in half, keeping the fold along the straight edge of the design. Don't worry if the edges of the paper aren't straight. You will trim the vellum later with a paper cutter. With scissors, cut along the wavy edge of the vellum, cutting off the small flowers to get a smooth flowing line.

three »

APPLY TAPE TO CARD | Place a strip of vellum tape along the top fold of the peach card. Burnish the tape down, and remove the backing off the tape.

four »

INSERT VELLUM | Place the stamped vellum on the table. Insert the fold of the peach card into the fold of the vellum and press to secure.

five »

COLOR THE DRAGONFLY | Using a paper cutter, trim the card and vellum sides to the edge of the stamped design. Stamp the dragonfly image onto the smaller piece of vellum and heat emboss as before. With scissors, cut out the dragonfly image, cutting off the antennae. Color in the wings on the back side of the vellum with the coral brush marker.

six »

EMBOSS THE DRAGONFLY SECTIONS | Place the dragonfly face down on the embossing pad. Dip the large end of the stylus into the wax, then run the stylus over the areas of the dragonfly that you'd like to dry emboss. For this project, I chose to emboss the edges of the wings and the body.

seven »

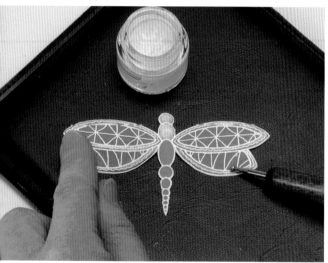

TURN OVER TO CHECK PROGRESS | You can see from this front view of the dragonfly that I've embossed the top section of the body and will begin to emboss the back of the rest of the body.

eight »

ADHERE DRAGONFLY TO THE CARD | Place vellum tape at the base of each wing near the body, and attach the dragonfly to the card.

Tip! **When dry embossing larger areas of a project, it is best to use a circular motion beginning at the outer edges and working inward. With practice, you will soon learn how to add an even and solid-looking whiteness to your vellum paper.**

CREATE DRAGONFLY ANTENNAE | Bend the 4" (10cm) length of wire into a V shape. Clasp one end of the wire in the round-nose pliers and turn the pliers to make a curl for the antenna. Clasp the other end of the wire and curl the end for the second antenna.

GLUE ANTENNAE TO THE HEAD | Place a bit of clear-drying craft glue under the head of the dragonfly and slip the antennae under the head into the glue.

ADD RHINESTONES | Squirt a puddle of glue onto some scrap paper. Dip one end of a toothpick into the glue and place a small dot of glue onto the dragonfly wing where you would like to apply a rhinestone. Dip the other end of the toothpick into water and touch that end to a rhinestone. The water will act like a magnet and pick up the rhinestone. Then place it onto the dot of glue on the dragonfly. Place three rhinestones on each wing. Allow to dry.

Tip! **When cutting down paper that has a heat-embossed image, if any of the embossing cracks as you cut, just reheat the edges with the heat gun to melt the embossing powder again.**

In this chapter we will explore the art of theorem painting to create a card and photo mat that look as if a professional artist has hand-painted the design. This technique dates back to the earlier half of the nineteenth century and was popular among aspiring artists of all ages. The composition of a theorem painting is achieved by using a series of stencils that are cut in such a way that no two areas immediately adjacent to one another can be on the same stencil. This process of multiple stencils produces a seamless image.

You will find great success in completing wonderful projects using overlay stencils to create these effects. The use of oil paint and small stencil brushes will allow you to attain the highlighting and shading that is critical to accomplish a realistic image. Please take the time to try out this extraordinary technique that will truly amaze your family and friends!

Overlay Stenciling

ELEGANT ROSE CARD

BUNNY PHOTO FRAME

STENCILING
B A S I C S

Materials

Overlay stencils are multiple-layer stencils that can be used to create a custom hand-painted look on a variety of surfaces. Generally, we think of stencils as being a single layer that creates a picture or pattern that has breaks and bridges. By utilizing overlay stencils, we can create a picture that has no breaks or bridges. Each stencil layer contains portions of the image that, when combined with other layers, create a complete image.

SMALL STENCIL BRUSHES
Small stencil brushes that measure ¼" to ⅜" (6mm to 10mm) in diameter work best for creating a lot of detail, like those that will be used in the projects in this chapter.

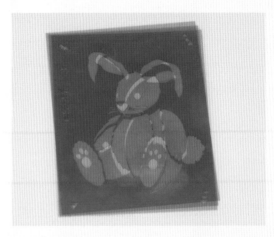

OIL STICKS
Oil sticks are a solid form of oil paint. Each time you use a color, you need to remove the hard skim at the top of the paint stick to expose the fresh, soft oil paint inside. Rub a bit of color onto the slick side of freezer paper or palette paper. This will serve as a paint palette, from which to pick up the paint. After about twenty-four hours, a skim will again form over the top of the paint stick.

OTHER ITEMS TO HAVE ON HAND

FREEZER PAPER OR PALETTE PAPER can be used as a palette for fresh paint. I prefer using something disposable, since oil paint is a bit messy to clean up.

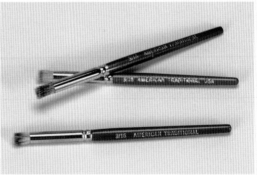

DRAFTING TAPE is a low-tack tape used to hold a stencil layer in place. It's also used under registration holes to make a mark on, rather than directly on the paper where the image will be.

PAPER TOWELS are a necessity when working with oils, for cleaning your hands and other surfaces.

DISHWASHING LIQUID is used to clean your brushes. A small amount of this soap on a clean spot of palette paper works well. Be sure to rinse your stencil brush well afterward, in hot water.

Techniques

Before getting started, you will need some tips and a rundown of how overlay stenciling works. Here are some helpful hints.

» Oil paint is permanent and will not come out of your clothing or carpet. On this note, apply color lightly. You cannot remove any applied paint, but you can always add more!

» Oil paints dry slowly. This allows you time to do some of your color mixing. You should have one stencil brush for each color; otherwise the paint will mix right on the brush, creating some colors you may not want.

» Pick up paint off of the palette in a swirling motion, then swirl on a clean spot on the palette paper to evenly distribute the paint throughout the brush. Apply paint to the project using the same swirling motion. Experiment with light and heavy pressure to obtain different color values.

» Get comfortable with the color wheel. Remember the basic combinations you learned in kindergarten? With just the three primary colors plus black and white, you can create virtually any color and any shade.

one »

REMOVE SKIM | Using a paper towel, remove the skim from the top of the oil stick.

two »

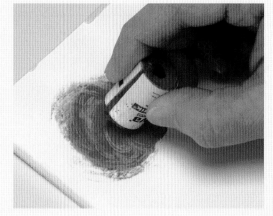

PREPARE PALETTE | Swirl each color to be used onto the palette paper. Leave enough room between the colors to prevent unwanted blending. Be sure to have a separate brush ready for each color.

three »

SECURE THE FIRST STENCIL | Stencils are numbered; use them in numerical order. Use drafting tape along the top of the first stencil to secure it to the paper. Apply a small piece of tape under each triangular registration mark, then on the tape, mark each triangle with a pencil, to allow registration for all of the layers.

four »

LOAD BRUSHES WITH COLOR | Swirl each brush around in its own color to get oil paint onto the brush.

five »

APPLYING GREEN | Apply green paint in a swirling motion to the areas of the daisy that are green. Use the illustration that came with the stencil packaging as a guide, if desired.

six »

ADD A LITTLE BLUE AND YELLOW | Apply blue oil paint directly on top of the green paint to accent the leaves. Next, color in the petals with yellow.

seven »

SHADE THE PETALS | Give the petals a little shading with some red paint here and there.

eight »

BLEND TOGETHER YELLOW AND RED | Add more yellow to the center of the daisy petals to further blend the red shading. Remove stencil 1 and wipe off the excess oil paint with a paper towel.

nine »

ALIGN STENCIL 2 | Using the triangle registration marks, secure stencil 2 and paint in the same manner as for stencil 1. When done, remove the stencil and wipe off excess paint.

ALIGN STENCIL 3 | Align stencil 3 with the registration marks as before and continue coloring in the daisy.

CREATE THE DAISY CENTER | For the daisy center, switch to brown and add color a little heavier around the perimeter.

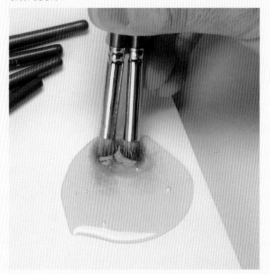

CLEAN BRUSHES | Clean brushes with dishwashing liquid. Put a little puddle on the palette paper and swirl each brush around until the paint comes off. Wash out the paint and soap with water in the sink and let the brushes dry completely before using them again.

ADD RED HIGHLIGHTS | Create highlights in the daisy center, using red. Remove stencil 3 and wipe clean.

elegant rose CARD

This beautiful rose card features a classic rose overlay stencil prepared on cream cardstock. The rose is further highlighted as a cutout oval with portions of the rose protruding from the oval. Hunter green and gold papers really add to the dramatic effect along with gold wired ribbon and paper-punched scalloped photo corners.

materials

- hunter green cardstock (2 sheets)
- cream cardstock
- gold metallic paper
- oil sticks
  alizarin crimson
  naphthol red
  prussian blue
  sap green
- 18" (46cm) of wired ¾" (19mm) gold ribbon
- drafting tape
- glue stick
- double-stick tape
- palette paper
- pencil
- ³⁄₁₆" (5mm) stencil brushes (4)
- paper towels
- dishwashing liquid
- craft knife
- cutting mat
- brayer

- scalloped photo corner paper punch
- ¼" (6mm) hole punch
- small scissors
- classic rose overlay stencil
- oval template 3" x 4" (7.6cm × 10.2cm)

PAPER PREPARATION »

Trim the following papers to the given sizes:

hunter green cardstock: 10" x 7" (254mm x 178mm) folded to 5" x 7" (127mm x 178mm), 4" x 5¼" (102mm x 133mm)

cream cardstock: 4¼" x 5½" (108mm x 140mm)

gold metallic paper: 4¼" x 5½" (108mm x 140mm), 4" x 3" (102mm x 76mm)

one »

BEGIN WITH THE FIRST STENCIL | Prepare your paint palette. Tape the first stencil layer to the cream cardstock and create registration marks as directed in the Techniques section on page 43. Color the leaves with sap green as the base color and then add prussian blue for shading. Use the packaging picture for reference, if you wish. Add naphthol red to the tips of the leaves to achieve brown. Clean the naphthol red brush with a paper towel to remove blue and green oil paint from the brush. Use naphthol red as a base color of the rose. Add alizarin crimson to shade. Remove stencil 1. Wipe the stencil clean with a paper towel.

two »

ALIGN THE SECOND STENCIL | Align stencil 2 onto the cream cardstock using the registration marks as your guide. Color in the leaves with sap green as the base color and then add prussian blue for shading. Add naphthol red to the tips of the leaves to achieve brown. Clean the naphthol red brush with a paper towel to remove blue and green oil paint from the brush. Again use naphthol red for the base color of the rose. Use alizarin crimson for shading. Remove stencil 2. Wipe the stencil clean with a paper towel.

three »

ALIGN STENCIL 3 | Align stencil 3 onto the cream cardstock, using the registration marks as your guide. Color in the leaves with sap green as the base color and then add prussian blue for shading. Add naphthol red to the tips of the leaves to achieve brown. Clean the naphthol red brush with a paper towel to remove blue and green oil paint from the brush. Again use naphthol red for the base color of the rose. Use alizarin crimson for shading. Remove stencil 3. Wipe the stencil clean with a paper towel.

four »

COMPLETE THE ROSE IMAGE |
After completing stencil 3, check to make sure all the areas of the image are shaded correctly. Place any of the three stencils back on top of the image to add additional shading and definition. Clean the brushes in dishwashing liquid and set aside to dry.

five »

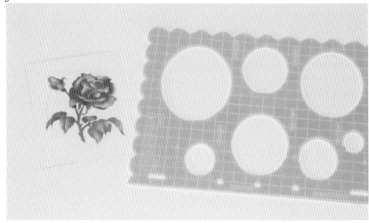

CREATE AN OVAL AROUND THE ROSE | Position the oval template over the rose image. Some of the image will be outside the oval. With a pencil, trace the oval, being careful to not mark on the colored portions.

six »

seven »

Tip! **When using a brayer over a painted image, it's a good idea to place a piece of scrap paper between the brayer and the image to prevent any smearing of the paint.**

ADHERE TO GREEN CARDSTOCK | Use a craft knife and the cutting mat, or a small pair of scissors to carefully cut out the oval and the parts of the image outside the oval. Use a brayer and a glue stick to adhere the rose image onto a 4" x 5¼" (10.2cm x 13.3cm) piece of hunter green cardstock.

CREATE PHOTO CORNERS | Use a scalloped photo corner punch to punch out four corners from the smaller piece of gold metallic paper. Use a glue stick to adhere each corner and fold the tabs onto the back of the cardstock. Use the brayer to make sure everything lies flat.

eight »

LAYER ONTO THE CARD | Center the layered rose image onto the larger piece of gold metallic. Use double-stick tape to adhere. Then attach all layers onto the folded hunter green card, using double-stick tape. Use a brayer to smooth everything down.

nine »

PUNCH THE HOLES | Use ¼" (6mm) hole punch on the fold of the card to punch four half circles. Use the edge of the gold metallic paper layer and the edge of the photo corner as your placement guide.

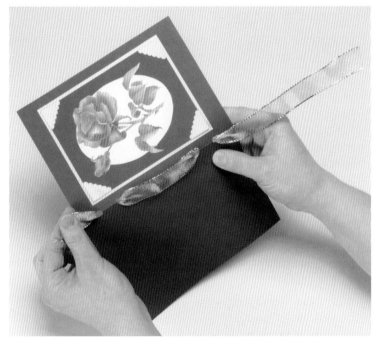

ten »

THREAD THE RIBBON | Thread the gold ribbon as shown along the fold of the card. Leave the ribbon ends out.

eleven »

TIE KNOTS AND TRIM TO FINISH | To create ribbon knots, thread each end under the center ribbon and then loop back through itself, forming a slipknot. Finish off the ribbon edges by cutting them at an angle with scissors.

bunny PHOTO FRAME

This bunny photo mat is so adorable! What a great way to display a picture of a child in a frame or use in a scrapbook. The checkerboard background colors could be changed to shades of blue for a boy, shades of pink for a girl, or bright and cheerful Easter colors. This is another easy project that will make you look like a pro!

materials

- light green cardstock
- white cardstock
- oil sticks
  - black
  - burnt umber
  - celedon green
  - medium pink
  - wedgewood blue
- 8" (20.3cm) of ¼" (6mm) light-green ribbon
- drafting tape
- craft-size Glue Dots
- double-stick tape
- palette paper
- pencil

- ³⁄₁₆" (5mm) stencil brushes (5)
- paper towels
- dishwashing liquid
- ruler
- craft knife
- cutting mat
- scissors
- paper cutter
- Creative Hot Marks tool (Walnut Hollow, optional)
- bunny overlay stencil
- checkerboard stencil
- 8" x 10" (20.3cm x 25.4cm) ready-made frame

PAPER PREPARATION »

Trim the following papers to the given sizes:

light green cardstock: 8" x 10" (20.3cm x 25.4cm)

white cardstock: 8" x 10" (20.3cm x 25.4cm)

one »

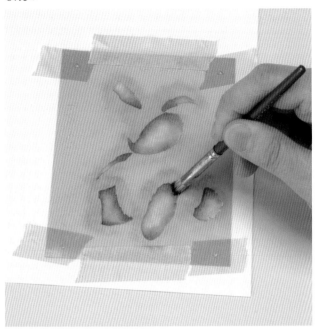

BEGIN WITH THE FIRST STENCIL | Prepare your palette and, using drafting tape, place stencil 1 of the bunny stencil in the lower right corner of the white cardstock. Add registration marks. Following the reference picture in the stencil packaging, begin with burnt umber paint. Working in a circular motion, apply the paint to the edges of the stencil openings and work the paint in toward the center of the opening. Darken the edges further with black paint.

two »

ALIGN STENCIL 2 | Remove stencil 1 and wipe off the excess paint with a paper towel. Place stencil 2 on the white cardstock, matching up the registration marks. Place a piece of drafting tape at the top of the stencil to hold it in place. Again, apply the burnt umber paint first, keeping the edges dark and working in toward the center. Apply black, lightly, in the same way.

three »

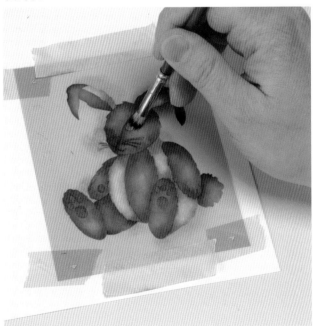

ALIGN STENCIL 3 | Remove stencil 2 and wipe off the excess paint with a paper towel. Tape stencil 3 in place, matching up the registration marks. Apply the burnt umber paint in a circular motion, then apply the black paint. Although the cutouts for the whiskers and pads seem small, the paint does get applied to the paper when you work in a circular motion.

four »

PREPARE CHECKERBOARD | Remove and clean stencil 3. Remove the tape from around the bunny. Place the checkerboard stencil in the upper left corner of the white cardstock, taping it into place. This stencil has no registration markings. You will use the checkerboard pattern for alignment.

BEGIN PAINTING SQUARES | Randomly fill in the checkerboard squares, using one color at time. Fill in several squares with the pink, then move on to the green, and then blue. Work the brush in a circular motion, and don't worry if some of the colors overlap.

STENCIL TO THE LEFT OF BUNNY | Remove the stencil and wipe it clean. Match the checkerboard pattern each time you move the stencil. Continue filling in the squares with random color. Wipe the stencil clean after each use. When you get to the bunny, place the stencil over the bunny and fill in the squares to the left of the bunny. You do not need to get real close. This section will ultimately be cut away.

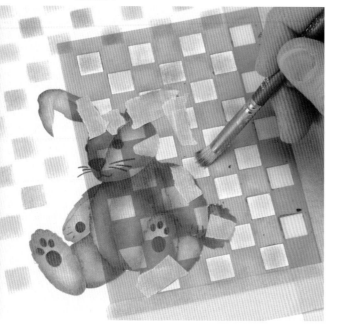

MASK OFF THE BUNNY | Remove the stencil and wipe it clean, then place the stencil over the bunny to the right side. Use drafting tape to mask off areas of the bunny. Then randomly fill in the squares as before. Use a light touch in the areas that are masked so that the color is soft and feathered.

CUT OUT THE WINDOW OPENING | Remove the stencil and wipe it clean, then finish the rest of the checkerboard background. Mask off areas of the bunny as needed. Clean the brushes in dishwashing liquid. Determine the size of the window opening by using the squares as guides. For this piece, my opening will be 4¾" x 6¼" (12.1cm x 16cm). You can make your opening a standard size if you prefer. Mark the area to be trimmed with a ruler and pencil. Trim the straight lines with a ruler and craft knife on the cutting mat.

TRIM AROUND THE BUNNY | Cut around the bunny with scissors. First, cut off the excess paper in the center, then cut closely around the bunny. Since the whiskers are so small and difficult to cut around, I just went ahead and cut them off.

TRIM TO FINISHED SIZE | Determine the size of the outer border, again using the squares as a guide. I decided to have a border of three squares on the top and bottom and two squares on the sides of the inside opening. Trim the border with a paper cutter or mark the border with a ruler and pencil and trim with the craft knife. Tie the ribbon in a bow, then adhere it to the bunny with a Glue Dot.

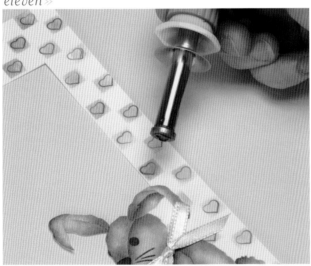

ADD HOT MARKS (OPTIONAL) | If you wish, use the Creative Hot Marks tool to burn a design onto each of the squares. Heat the tool and hold it to the square for about three seconds to create the design. The designs will not be completely uniform, but that just adds to the charm of the piece.

Tip! **Stenciling with a checkerboard pattern makes it easy to create a multiple-opening mat, for smaller cropped photos. The pattern acts like a graph, allowing you to easily cut out windows that are the same size and nicely aligned with one another.**

twelve

LAYER BUNNY ONTO GREEN CARDSTOCK | Mount the finished bunny photo mat on the light green cardstock with double-stick tape. Place tape along the bottom and two sides of the mat. Remember, you must leave one side open for the picture to be inserted into the photo mat. Insert a photo and then place the finished piece into the ready-made frame.

Originally a Dutch papercraft of the nineteenth century, this Victorian art form used to be quite time-consuming. All patterns had to measured out by hand. Times have changed! Now, there are a variety of metal piercing templates on the market that allow you to pierce patterns into paper in no time.

You can easily vary the look of your project by varying your type of paper. Soft and subtle effects are the result of lighter-weight papers, while metallic cardstock can give you the look of punched tin. This simple technique will produce gorgeous results every time!

Paper Piercing

FAUX TIN CARD

LAYERED PAPER ART

PIERCING
BASICS

Materials

The materials used for the projects in this chapter are all made specifically for paper piercing, and each makes the process just a bit easier. This technique is so simple, however, that it can be done with pushpins, foam core and your own pattern.

METAL PIERCING TEMPLATE
Each metal template contains a series of open holes that will produce a pattern when punched. Some metal templates also contain areas that can be cut out or dry embossed, such as the templates shown here.

PIERCING PAD
A piercing pad is a soft but dense pad that you place underneath the paper that is being pierced. This pad will protect your work surface.

PIERCING NEEDLE TOOL
A piercing needle tool has a tapered needle at the end. It is used for piercing the paper and is inserted into the holes of the template.

Techniques

The techniques used to pierce paper are as simple as the list of materials. If you wish to create even more variation in texture, choose a part of the pattern to punch in the opposite direction. Punch the desired amount of holes in one direction, then turn the paper over, and with the aid of a light box, reposition the template, secure it, and punch the remaining holes.

one»

POSITION TEMPLATE AND PUNCH HOLES | Center the piercing template on the paper and secure all four corners with drafting tape. Trace around the outside of the template with a pencil. Using the piercing needle tool, pierce all the holes.

two»

CUT OUT CENTER SHAPE | The center may be cut out with a craft knife and cutting mat, using the metal piercing template as a guide.

three»

REMOVE TEMPLATE | Remove the drafting tape and the template from the paper. Using the pencil marks as a guide, trim the paper on the paper cutter. Flip over to view finished piece.

Tip! **Some papers are thinner than others, so it may be possible to punch through two or more layers at a time. If several layers are desired, use paper that is slightly larger than your template and staple the layers together to keep them from shifting.**

faux tin CARD

This card really does have the look of punched tin. I used metallic silver paper and metallic rub–ons to achieve this effect. I was also able to punch through several layers at one time because the metallic paper I used was fairly thin, so I had the makings for several cards after punching the design only once.

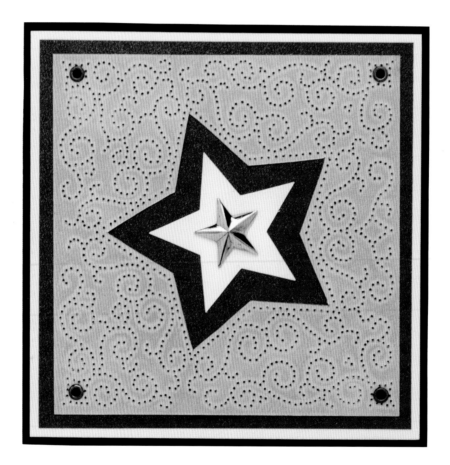

materials

- plum cardstock
- light ivory cardstock
- silver metallic paper
- plum metallic paper
- Silver Metallic Rub-Ons (Craf-T Products)
- four plum eyelets
- silver star charm
- drafting tape
- double-stick tape
- glue stick
- clear-drying craft glue
- piercing pad

- pencil
- piercing needle tool
- craft knife
- cutting mat
- paper cutter
- scrap paper
- small star punch
- ⅛" (3mm) hole punch
- eyelet setting tool
- hammer
- protective surface for hammering
- 4⅝" (11.7cm) star paper piercing template

PAPER PREPARATION »

Trim the following papers to the given sizes:

plum cardstock: 11" x 5½"(28cm x 14cm) folded to 5½" x 5½" (14cm x 14cm)

light ivory cardstock: 5¼" x 5¼" (13.3cm x 13.3cm), 3" x 3" (7.6cm x 7.6cm)

silver metallic paper: 5½" x 5½" (14cm x 14cm), (several, if you would like to pierce more than one layer)

plum metallic paper: 5" x 5" (12.7cm x 12.7cm)

one »

APPLY RUB-ONS TO PIERCED STAR | Using the piercing template and the silver metallic paper, complete the piercing and cut out of the star (see page 57). Trim the piece to 4⅜" x 4⅜" (11.2cm x 11.2cm). Place the pierced piece of paper, raised side up, on a piece of scrap paper. Using the silver metallic rub-on, rub silver over the piece in a circular fashion with your finger. This will give the piece more of a metallic look. Set aside to dry.

two »

LAYER THE STAR AND OTHER PAPERS | Use double-stick tape to layer the larger piece of light ivory cardstock onto the front of the plum fold-over card. Using glue stick, layer the plum metallic paper, then dab glue stick onto the back of the pierced piece and layer it onto the plum paper.

three »

ADD SECOND STAR AND EYELETS | Punch one star out of the smaller piece of light ivory cardstock and adhere it to the center of the pierced star opening, using a glue stick. Use a ⅛" (3mm) hole punch to punch one hole out of each corner of the layered piece. Secure the four plum eyelets, using the eyelet setting tool, hammer and protective surface (refer to the Basic Techniques section on page 14). Adhere the silver star charm with clear-drying craft glue in the center of the light ivory star. Allow to dry.

layered paper ART

Creating pictures for your home is inexpensive and a lot of fun. In this project I used coordinating scrapbooking paper, metallic paper and cardstock to create a layered-paper piece of art. I used a square-shaped template for this piece, but any small shape would work fine. I just love the way these mini gold rhinestones add a touch of sparkle!

materials

- cream cardstock (2 sheets)
- gold metallic paper (2 sheets)
- coordinating scrapbook paper
    leaf paper (2 sheets)
    plaid paper
- matboard (optional)
- olive pastel ink pad
- gold rhinestones (5)
- metal corners (4)
- drafting tape
- glue stick
- ⅛" (3mm) foam tape
- clear-drying craft glue
- waxed paper

- lightbox
- stylus
- piercing pad
- piercing needle tool
- deckle-edged scissors
- brayer
- scrap paper
- small cup of water
- toothpick
- 1½" (3.8cm) square metal piercing and embossing template
- 8" x 10" (20.3cm x 25.4cm) gold frame

PAPER PREPARATION »

Trim the following papers to the given sizes:

cream cardstock: 8" x 10" (20.3cm x 25.4cm), 2½" x 2½" (6.4cm x 6.4cm) (5 total)

gold metallic paper: 6¼" x 8¼" (16cm x 21cm), 5" x 5" (12.7cm x 12.7cm), 3¾" x 3¾" (9.5cm x 9.5cm)

coordinating scrapbook paper:
- leaf paper: 8" x 10" (20.3cm x 25.4cm), 4¾" x 4¾" (12.1cm x 12.1cm)
- plaid paper: 6" x 8" (15.2cm x 20.3cm)

matboard (optional): ³⁄₁₆" x 10" (5mm x 25.4cm) (4 total), ³⁄₁₆" x 7½" (5mm x 19.1cm) (4 total)

one »

EMBOSS AND PIERCE IVORY PIECES | Dry emboss one of the five small pieces of ivory cardstock with the metal template (see dry embossing techniques, page 31). With the stencil still taped to the paper, place it onto the piercing pad (metal template side up). Using the piercing needle tool, pierce all the holes, taking care to remove one piece of drafting tape at a time when necessary to avoid punching through it.

two »

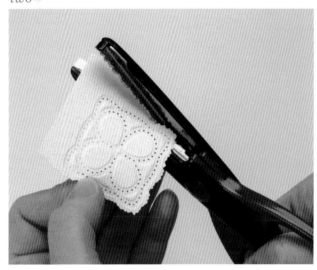

TRIM WITH DECKLE-EDGED SCISSORS | Remove the stencil and, using the deckle-edged scissors, cut the shape out, leaving about ⅛" (3mm) border outside of the embossed line. Repeat dry embossing, piercing, and deckle cutting with the other four pieces of ivory cardstock.

three »

DIP EDGES INTO OLIVE INK | Dip the edges of each piece into the olive pastel ink pad. Set aside to dry.

four »

LAYER BACKGROUND PIECES | Apply glue stick to the back of the large piece of leaf paper and adhere to the large piece of cream cardstock. Layer the large piece of gold metallic paper to the leaf paper, using a glue stick, followed by the plaid paper. Next, center and adhere the medium piece of gold metallic paper on the diagonal to the plaid paper, followed by the small piece of leaf paper and the small piece of gold metallic paper. Brayer down all layers.

five »

ARRANGE PIERCED PIECES | Distribute four of the pierced pieces evenly onto the gold metallic paper. Dab glue stick onto each and adhere. Apply five small pieces of the ⅛" (3mm) foam tape to each corner and in the center of the final pierced piece and center it on a diagonal over the other four pierced pieces.

six »

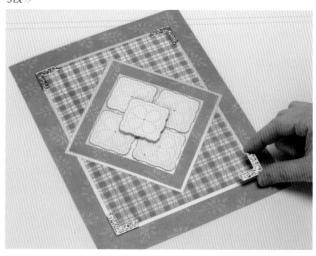

ADD RHINESTONES | Squirt a puddle of clear-drying craft glue onto some scrap paper. Dip one end of a toothpick into the glue and place a small dot onto the center of a pierced square. Dip the other end of the toothpick into water and touch that end to a rhinestone. The water acts like a magnet to pick up the rhinestone. Place the rhinestone onto the dot of glue on the pierced square. Adhere one rhinestone to the center of each of the five pieces. Using the clear-drying craft glue, adhere one metal corner to all four corners of the larger gold metallic paper. Let dry.

CONVERT A STANDARD FRAME TO A SHADOW-BOX FRAME

The following two steps will need to be completed if you are using a standard frame, and you wish to create the look of a shadow-box. You could omit these steps if you use a shadow-box frame or if you wish to display your piece without glass.

one »

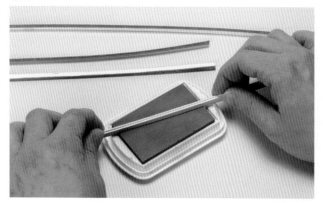

CREATE SHADOW-BOX STRIPS | Using glue stick, glue together two pieces of each length of matboard, making a double thickness of matboard. This will leave you with a total of four pieces. Dip one long side of each of the mat board strips into the olive pastel ink pad. Set aside to dry.

two »

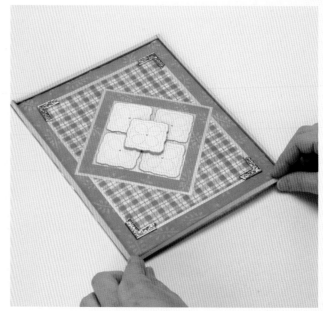

ADD STRIPS TO THE FRAME | Using clear-drying craft glue, adhere the two 10" (25.4cm) lengths to the outside of the two long sides of the piece. Adhere the 7½" (19.1cm) lengths to the outside of the short sides. Secure strips with clips while the glue dries. The finished piece is now ready to put into the frame.

variation

PHOTO MAT

USE A GREEN METALLIC RUB-ON

This pretty pierced piece serves as a lovely mat for this photo frame. To create this look, I used a template that had a nice open circle in its center. After punching out the design, I had a great place to add my photo. I then used Metallic Green Rub-On to add color over the entire piece. The punched areas naturally resists the color, creating contrast and depth. The simple bow and wording at the bottom balances things out nicely.

Tip! **When working with metallic rub-ons, apply the first amount with your finger lightly to avoid getting a fingerprint. Then buff the color with your finger as you apply more and more color, to give your project a shiny metal look.**

Quilling, or paper filigree, is the art of rolling paper strips into shapes and then using the shapes to form various designs and images. It has been around since the time of the Renaissance period, which goes to show the materials and supplies needed are not complicated or hard to come by.

Originally, European cloisters or religious orders would have been the only groups with access to the handmade papers that were used in this art, but today you can even buy bags of strips that are accurately cut by machine and ready to use. I prefer to cut my own strips because then I'm not limited by the paper I can use, but if time is precious, the option of precut paper is available to you.

In this chapter you will learn how to use paper strips, glue and a needle tool to create elegant floral embellishments for your paper crafting projects. I will teach you how to make a five-petal flower and a rose, both adorned with leaves. After you learn these simple techniques, I'm sure you will want to discover more of the world of quilling!

Quilling

BASKET OF FLOWERS

LACE HEART CARD

QUILLING
BASICS

Materials

While the basic materials needed for quilling might be minimal, let's discuss a few specifics before you begin rolling! Lightweight paper tends to work better than a heavier paper because it is easier to manipulate its memory, or tendency to curl in a direction all its own.

WORKBOARD AND STRAIGHT PINS

It is wonderful to have some assistance while quilling by using a quilling workboard and straight pins. My favorite workboard has an area to pin my project together on, as well as various sizes of circles to help me keep my quilled circles even. You can also create your own workboard out of foamboard or corkboard.

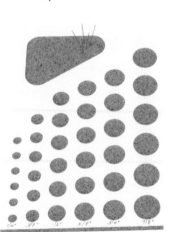

SLOTTED TOOL AND NEEDLE TOOL

Use either a slotted tool or a needle tool to roll up your paper strips. Instructions for using them are described on page 67.

PAPER QUILLING STRIPS

Strips for quilling can be purchased in an assortment of colors already precut to a specific width. You may also cut your own strips on the paper cutter, making sure to use lightweight paper. Standard paper widths are ⅛" (3mm), ¼" (6mm), ⅜" (10mm), ½" (13mm) and ⅝" (16mm).

ADDITIONAL ITEMS YOU WILL NEED

CLEAR-DRYING CRAFT GLUE Craft glue is thick enough to not run all over your project and it will dry clearly and quickly.

MOIST WASHCLOTH Your needle tool works well to apply glue to your quilled pieces, so keep a moist washcloth on hand to wipe off the needle tool after applying glue.

FINE-POINTED TWEEZERS Fine pointed tweezers are helpful for grasping the small quilled components used in making a particular design.

FREEZER PAPER OR PALETTE PAPER Use one of these items as a palette for glue. Use only a small amount of glue at a time because the glue dries very quickly. The freezer paper or palette paper can also be used to protect the cork area of your workboard while quilled pieces are being glued together.

Techniques

Two needle tools available for quilling will be used for this chapter's projects. The difference between them, as well as a word on gluing, is worth a quick mention here.

Using the Slotted Tool »

The slotted tool is easier for most people to learn to quill with. The end of a quilling strip is inserted into a slot, which holds the paper securely.

INSERT THE STRIP INTO THE SLOT | Place the paper into the slot, just to the edge. Roll the paper. When the strip is completely rolled up, pull the rolled strip off of the tool and place it on the table. Allow the strip to unfurl, and then glue the rolled paper according to the project directions.

T i p ! **Avoid using your slotted tool to apply glue. The glue can clog the slotted end of the tool.**

Using the Needle Tool »

The needle tool has a straight metal tip on which to roll your quilling paper. This tool will make smaller centers when creating your quilled pieces than the slotted tool and requires just a bit of practice to use.

one »

HOLD THE STRIP TO THE NEEDLE | Moisten the tip of the paper just slightly with your tongue. Place the paper behind the needle tool with the edge of the paper strip just slightly over the length of the needle.

two »

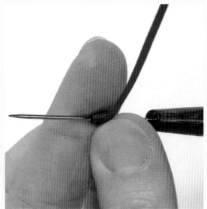

ROLL THE PAPER | Roll the paper strip tightly between your thumb and index finger. When the strip is completely rolled up, pull the rolled strip off of the tool and place it on the table. Allow the strip to unfurl. Glue the rolled paper according to the desired size.

three »

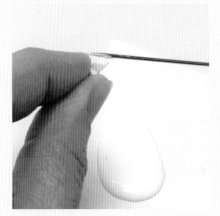

APPLY GLUE | Place a puddle of glue onto your palette paper. Dip your needle tool into the glue and place a bit of glue on the loose end of the rolled paper. Hold the paper for a short time to seal the rolled shape. Wipe the needle tool clean on a moist washcloth to remove the excess glue.

basket of FLOWERS

Quilling can be time-consuming, but this project uses a rubber-stamped basket, a paper-punched basket cloth, a dragonfly metal charm and only a few quilled flowers to create a lovely framed piece for your home. I am sure once you learn how to produce these simple flowers and leaves, you will think of a multitude of projects they could be used in.

materials

- ivory cardstock
- woodgrain or tan cardstock
- metallic burgundy paper
- metallic green paper
- gold paper
- Memories Artprint Brown ink pad (Stewart Superior)
- small dragonfly charm
- clear-drying craft glue
- glue stick
- mini Glue Dots
- needle tool and/or slotted tool
- palette paper
- moist washcloth
- quilling workboard
- straight pins
- brayer
- scissors
- 1¾" (4.5cm) square scalloped paper punch
- fine-pointed tweezers
- key basket rubber stamp
- 5" x 7" (12.7cm x 17.8cm) frame

PAPER PREPARATION »

Trim the following papers to the given sizes:

ivory cardstock: 5½" x 3½" (14cm x 9cm)

woodgrain or tan cardstock: 3½" x 3¼" (9cm x 8.3cm)

metallic burgundy paper: 5" x 7" (12.7cm x 17.8cm), ⅛" x 6" (3mm x 15.2cm) (15 total)

metallic green paper: 5¾" x 3¾" (14.6cm x 9.5cm), 2½" x 2½" (6.4cm x 6.4cm), ⅛" x 6" (3mm x 15.2cm) (9 total)

gold paper: ⅛" x 3" (3mm x 7.6cm) (3 total)

ROLL FLOWER PETALS AND CENTERS | Use either the needle tool or the slotted tool to make three tight rolls of the gold paper strips for the flower centers. Use clear-drying craft glue to secure the ends. Roll a piece of 6" (15.2cm) burgundy paper tightly, then place it into the ⅜" (10mm) hole on the workboard and let it unfurl to the size of the hole. Repeat for a total of five burgundy pieces.

PINCH PETAL ROLLS | Glue the ends of each piece to secure. Holding the paper near the seam, pinch the outer edge of one roll to create a teardrop-shaped petal. Repeat for the remaining four petals. Make ten more burgundy petals in this way so that you have enough for three flowers with five petals on each.

ROLL AND PINCH LEAVES | Make rolls of the 6" (15.2cm) green paper and place them in the ⅜" (10mm) hole on the workboard to unfurl. Glue the end of the paper. Pinch the seam end to create a teardrop shape like for the flower. To make this into a leaf shape, pinch the opposite end in the same way. Make two leaves for each flower and three more for placing throughout the arrangement.

four »

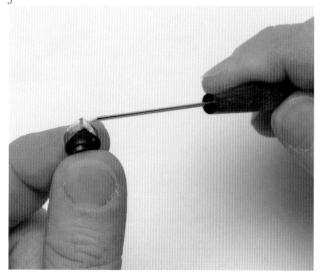

APPLY GLUE TO THE PETALS | To assemble the arrangement, begin by applying craft glue to both sides of the pinched part of a flower petal.

five »

SECURE THE PETAL TO WORKBOARD | Place the petal on the workboard and pin it to the board with two straight pins to keep it in place. Protect the cork with a piece of palette or freezer paper, if desired.

six »

CREATE FLOWER SHAPES | Repeat this process for the rest of the petals, gluing each and placing them next to each other to form the flower. Glue the center onto the flower by placing the glue on the bottom of the paper roll. Next, place two leaves by gluing the sides that will touch the flower petals. Allow the pieces to dry, then remove the pins. Repeat for the other two flower groupings.

LAYER BACKGROUND AND BASKET | Use the cardboard from the frame or cut your own piece to 5" x 7" (12.7cm x 17.8cm). Use a glue stick to mount the large piece of burgundy paper to the cardboard. Brayer the piece to secure. Glue the large sheet of green paper to the center of the burgundy, using the glue stick. Layer the ivory cardstock over the green paper and brayer to secure. Stamp the basket stamp onto the woodgrain or tan cardstock with the brown ink and use scissors to cut it out. Use a glue stick to adhere the basket to the center of the ivory cardstock.

ARRANGE FLOWERS IN THE BASKET | Punch one scalloped square out of the small piece of metallic green paper. Cut the square in half on the diagonal and use a glue stick to glue half onto the basket. Arrange the flower pieces on the right side of the basket in a way you find appealing. Insert some of the extra leaves if you wish. To glue the flower and leaf pieces onto the surface, dip your needle tool into the craft glue and tap it on the bottom of each piece. To apply glue onto the spiral centers of each piece, push the centers gently from the front and tap on some glue with your needle tool.

nine

> *Tip!* **To display your piece under glass, you could buy a shadow-box frame, or any frame with enough depth to hold your piece, or complete all steps up to gluing the flowers on and place the paper under the glass. Then glue the flowers and dragonfly on top of the glass. (For instructions on converting a regular frame into a shadow-box frame, see page 62.)**

ADD THE CHARM AND FRAME | Attach the dragonfly charm with a Glue Dot. Remove the glass from your frame, if it came with glass, and place your piece in the frame. Display with pride!

lace heart CARD

This project again uses basic rubber stamping and paper layering. I used the slotted quilling tool to fashion a quilled rose much like the ribbon roses you can purchase at your local craft store. This rose is easy to make out of a strip of paper and can be added to so many projects!

materials

- white cardstock
- silver cardstock
- vellum paper
- metallic lavender paper
- metallic green paper
- Brilliance Moonlight White ink pad (Tsukineko)
- clear-drying craft glue
- vellum tape

- craft-sized Glue Dots
- quilling workboard
- palette paper
- straight pins
- slotted quilling tool
- scissors
- deckle-edged scissors
- lace heart rubber stamp

PAPER PREPARATION »

Trim the following papers to the given sizes:

white cardstock: 11" x 5½" (28cm x 14cm) folded to 5½" x 5½" (14cm x 14cm)

silver cardstock: 4⅞" x 4⅞" (12.4cm x 12.4cm)

vellum paper: 4" x 4" (10.2cm x 10.2cm)

metallic lavender paper: 3⅞" x 3⅞" (9.8cm x 9.8cm), ⅜" x 11" (10mm × 28cm)

metallic green paper: 5⅛" x 5⅛" (13cm x 13cm), 4⅛" x 4⅛" (10.5cm x 10.5cm), ½" x 3" (13mm x 7.6cm) (3 total)

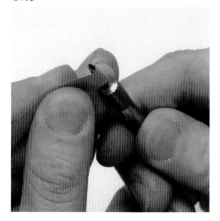

one

INSERT LAVENDER PAPER | Cover the cork on your quilling workboard with a small piece of palette paper or freezer paper to protect it from the glue. Place a small puddle of clear-drying craft glue on some palette paper and place your straight pins within reach of the workboard. Using the slotted tool and the lavender strip of paper, place the end of the strip into the tool and make three full counterclockwise turns and secure the roll with your thumb.

FOLD DOWN TO FORM A PETAL | Using your opposite hand, fold the strip down at approximately a 45° angle.

COMPLETE ONE TURN | Continue to turn the slotted tool counterclockwise until your thumb is at the end of the first fold. Secure the roll with your thumb to keep the roll from creeping forward. Keep the bottom edge of the lavender strip aligned, allowing the top edge to fan out.

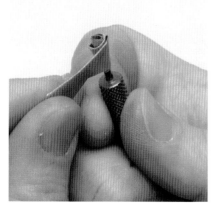

CONTINUE FOLDING | Make a second fold and turn again until your thumb is at the end of the fold. Secure the roll with your thumb. Repeat this process until approximately 2" (5.1cm) of paper is left.

RELEASE ROSE FROM THE TOOL | Release the roll and remove it from the slotted tool. (If the rose doesn't come off easily, you have wound it too tightly.) Lay the rose on the table and let it unfurl on its own.

EXPOSE THE INNER ROLL AND GLUE | Fold the paper tail back underneath the rose to form a base for gluing the rose. Push the center of the flower downward from the front to expose the inner folds of the rose underneath, and apply glue generously.

GLUE TO SECURE | Fold the paper tail onto the base of the rose, securing it into the glue.

SET THE ROSE ASIDE TO DRY | Pin the quilled rose to the workboard to secure it while the glue dries. Don't worry about the small holes from the pins. They will not show at all.

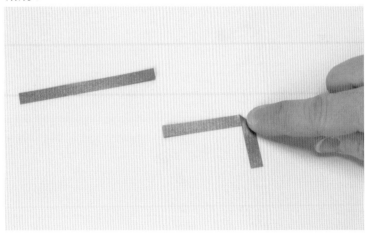

BEGIN FOLDING THE LEAF | Use a 3" (7.6cm) green strip of paper for each leaf. Make one right-angle fold.

CONTINUE FOLDING LEAVES | Make another right-angle fold on the opposite side, forming a triangular point. Repeat with the remaining green strips.

eleven »

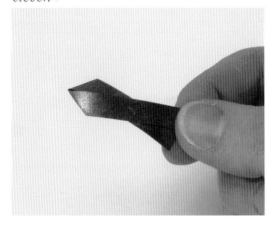

ADD DIMENSION TO THE LEAVES | Cross over the two ends of the excess paper so they overlap and add a curve to the leaf. Secure with glue and allow to dry. Cut off the excess paper strips with scissors. Repeat with the other two strips.

twelve »

ADD LEAVES TO THE ROSE | Glue the finished leaves to the bottom of the rose, overlapping them and spacing them out evenly.

thirteen »

LAYER AND COMPLETE THE CARD | Using glue stick, layer the large green paper, silver cardstock, medium green paper and large lavender paper to the white fold-over card. Ink the lace heart stamp with the white ink pad and stamp onto the vellum. Allow to dry and then use deckle-edged scissors to cut the heart out, leaving a narrow border. Adhere the heart to the layered card with vellum tape. Use a Glue Dot to adhere the rose to the top of the heart.

In this chapter you will explore paper casting, which is a form of making paper. When you make a paper cast, the basic supplies you will utilize are cotton linter, a blender, water and a mold. For the three projects that follow, a store-bought mold was used, but it is possible to create your own using plaster or polymer clay. The molds used for fancy cookies work just as well also.

As you will be able to see, paper casts are a versatile way to embellish greeting cards, gift bags and handmade photo albums and journals. This is a fun and yet totally different technique for paper. If you find yourself reveling in the papermaking process, you may wish to experiment with different additives to the cotton linter pulp, including various pigmented papers, fibers and glitter. So let's get those blenders out!

Paper Casting

MAGNOLIA CARD

GIFT BAG

PHOTO ALBUM

CASTING
BASICS

Materials

Before you begin casting your own creations, you will need to gather a few items to break the cotton linter down so that you can reshape it in the form of something else. This process uses a lot of water, so be prepared with some extra towels.

COTTON LINTERS
Cotton linters come in two forms, loose (resembles stuffing and comes in large bags) and prepressed squares. The squares are the form that will be used in this chapter. You will need to tear the squares into small pieces before using.

BLENDER
A blender is needed to prepare the paper pulp for molding. I recommend devoting a blender entirely to paper making. Some linters contain dye whose toxins can be absorbed by the blender and may contaminate food used in the blender in the future. Also, over time, the cotton fibers can dull the blades, making food preparation more difficult.

PAPER-CASTING MOLDS
Paper-casting molds come in many styles and sizes. Also be on the lookout for things that you might have around the house that are water resistant and could become a mold.

ADDITIONAL ITEMS YOU WILL NEED
RELEASE AGENT (NONSTICK COOKING SPRAY)
A release agent makes it easier to remove the paper casting from the mold. Spray the mold before adding the paper pulp.

SPONGES Sponges are used for removing excess water from the mold during the molding process.

OLD TOWELS Cover your molding area with old towels to soak up excess water.

SCRAPS OF PROCESSED PAPER Adding scraps of processed paper will introduce sizing into the paper casting which is important if you ever want to write on or color the paper you have cast. The use of colored paper will also introduce color.

STRAINER The blended pulp is poured through a strainer to remove excess water.

LARGE BOWL A large bowl will be needed to catch excess water as you strain the pulp.

Techniques

Even after I have done it for years, this process of whirling water and fibers in a blender and then ending up with a new form of paper still fascinates me. The strained pulp can be placed in a plastic zipper bag and frozen for about a month, if you end up with more than you need. Also, one neat thing about paper casting: If you don't like how your casting comes out, throw it back in the blender with more water and try something else!

one »

DETERMINE LINTER AMOUNT |
Take enough cotton linter to cover the mold you will be using. Add a piece of plain white copy paper the size of the mold to introduce sizing.

two »

TEAR AND ADD TO BLENDER |
Tear up the pieces and place them in the blender. Add a generous amount of water and allow the cotton linter to soak up some water. Blend for about one minute.

three »

STRAIN THE PULP | Prepare the mold by spraying lightly with a nonstick cooking spray. Holding the strainer over the large bowl, pour out the pulp mixture from the blender.

four »

POUR OFF THE EXCESS WATER |
Drain the majority of the water off, and place the wet pulp mixture into the mold. Using your hands, spread the pulp entirely over the mold.

five »

BLOT WATER WITH A SPONGE |
Take a sponge and apply pressure to the pulp to remove as much water as possible. Wring out the sponge and repeat several times. Let the molded paper dry several hours or overnight if needed.

six »

REMOVE CASTING FROM MOLD |
When the paper casting is dry, carefully pry it out of the mold. A butter knife works well if the casting needs a little coaxing.

magnolia CARD

This beautiful paper-cast magnolia looks great layered on printed vellum and burgundy cardstock. This is a fast and elegant card to put together once you have the paper casting all done. I left the magnolia untinted, but you could choose to add a bit of color to it if you wanted. Patterned vellum adds texture without detracting from the lovely flower.

materials

- burgundy cardstock (2 sheets)
- silver cardstock
- patterned vellum
- cotton linter squares
- white copy paper (for sizing)
- water
- vellum tape
- double-stick tape
- clear-drying craft glue
- blender
- nonstick cooking spray
- old towels
- strainer
- large bowl
- sponges
- paper cutter
- magnolia paper casting mold

PAPER PREPARATION

Trim the following papers to the given sizes:

burgundy cardstock: 11" x 8" (28cm x 20.3cm), folded to 5½" x 8" (14cm x 20.3cm), 3¼" x 3¼" (8.3cm x 8.3cm), 2" x 7" (5.1cm x 17.8cm)

silver cardstock: 3½" x 3½" (9cm x 9cm), 2¼" x 7" (5.7cm x 17.8cm)

patterned vellum: 11" x 8" (28cm x 20.3cm), folded to 5½" x 8" (14cm x 20.3cm), 1½" x 7" (3.8cm x17.8cm)

cotton linter squares: (enough to cover mold)

white copy paper (for sizing): 3" x 3" (7.6cm x 7.6cm)

CAST MAGNOLIA | Using the basic technique for creating a paper casting, create one paper-cast magnolia. Apply a line of vellum tape along the fold on the back of the burgundy fold-over card. Attach the folded vellum over the card.

two »

TRIM VELLUM AND BURGUNDY CARDSTOCK | Keeping the card and the vellum together, trim the three sides on the paper cutter to create a new card size of 5" x 7" (12.7cm x 17.8cm). Layer the silver strip down the center of the front of the card, using double-stick tape. Onto that, layer the burgundy strip and then finally, using vellum tape, layer the patterned vellum strip on top of the burgundy strip.

three »

ADD SILVER SQUARE AND MAGNOLIA | Using double-stick tape, adhere the burgundy square to the silver square, and then layer this on the diagonal in the center of the card. Adhere the paper casting, using craft glue, to the center of the burgundy square. Smooth the edges of the casting down. Set aside to dry.

Tip! **The use of colored paper will introduce color into the paper pulp mixture. The finished shade will be lighter than the original paper chosen.**

gift BAG

Custom gift bags are another great way to use paper castings. Coordinating scrapbooking paper and cardstock are used to embellish this plain, kraft gift bag. You can change the casting image to suit the occasion. The same papers would also look nice on a solid-colored bag that coordinated with the tones in the papers.

materials

- kraft paper gift bag
  8" x 10" x 5" (20.3cm x 25.4cm x 12.7cm)
- white cardstock (2 sheets)
- goldenrod cardstock
  (for sizing and color)
- coordinating scrapbook paper
  plaid print
  blue denim print (2 sheets)
- cotton linter squares (enough to cover the mold)
- bisque ink pad
- water
- glue stick
- clear-drying craft glue
- blender
- nonstick cooking spray
- old towels
- strainer
- large bowl
- sponges
- brayer
- cosmetic sponge
- daisy paper casting mold

PAPER PREPARATION »

Trim the following papers to the given sizes:

white cardstock: 3¾" x 3¾" (9.5cm x 9.5cm), 3¼" x 3¼" (8.3cm x 8.3cm), 2¾" x 6¾" (7cm x 17.2cm)

goldenrod cardstock: 1½" x 3" (3.8cm x 7.6cm)

coordinating scrapbook paper:
- plaid print: 6½" x 8½" (16.5cm x 21.6cm), 3½" x 3½" (9cm x 9cm), 2½" x 6½" (6.4cm x 16.5cm)
- blue denim print: 6¾" x 8¾" (17.2cm x 22.2cm), 4½" x 4½" (11.4cm x 11.4cm), 3½" x 7½" (9cm x 19.1cm)

one »

two »

CAST DAISY AND LAYER PAPERS ONTO BAG | Using the basic technique for paper casting, this time adding goldenrod cardstock in lieu of copy paper for color and sizing, create one daisy paper casting. Apply glue stick to the largest piece of blue denim paper and center it on the front of the kraft paper bag. Next, layer the largest plaid paper and then the medium blue denim print. Then layer the largest piece of white card stock, and then the medium-size plaid paper. Use a brayer to seal everything down.

LAYER PIECES FOR CAST DAISY | Use a glue stick to adhere the medium-size white card stock to the smallest blue denim print paper. Next, layer the smallest plaid print paper and the smallest white cardstock. Adhere this finished square piece on the diagonal to the center of the bag.

three »

four »

ADHERE DAISY TO THE BAG | Using clear-drying craft glue, adhere the finished paper casting to the center of the white cardstock square. Allow to dry.

APPLY BISQUE TO THE DAISY | Tear off the larger end of the cosmetic sponge and dab in the bisque ink pad. Apply this color in a dabbing fashion to the raised parts of the daisy paper casting.

Tip! **If the mold you are using is made of terra cotta, one way to speed up the drying time of wet pulp is to put it into the oven or microwave. Drying shouldn't be done too quickly, however, or the piece might warp. Keep oven temperature around 250° F (120° C), or microwave in one-minute intervals. Be sure to read the manufacturer's packaging regarding the safety of using a mold in the microwave or oven.**

photo ALBUM

In this project I created a mini photo album and journal. This is a great project to record that fishing, hiking or camping trip! This album has seven pages but can be modified to accommodate any number of pages.

materials

- cream cardstock (3 sheets)
- leaf green cardstock
- off-white sturdy textured paper
- gold metallic paper
- coordinating scrapbook paper
  green plaid print
  light brown natural print
- book boards or sturdy matboard
- cotton linter squares
- deep green ink pad
- raffia, 3–4 yards (3–4m), cut into 1 yard (1m) strands
- glue stick
- clear-drying craft glue
- blender
- nonstick cooking spray

- old towels
- strainer
- large bowl
- sponge
- brayer
- pencil
- scissors
- bone folder
- ½" (13mm) small pine tree paper punch
- scrap paper
- cutting mat
- cosmetic sponge
- ruler or straight edge
- trees paper casting mold

PAPER PREPARATION

Trim the following papers to the given sizes:

cream cardstock: 4¼" x 11" (10.8cm x 28cm), 4¼" x 5½" (10.8cm x 14cm) (7 total)

leaf green cardstock: 1½" x 3" (3.8cm x 7.6cm)

off-white sturdy textured paper: 3⅛" x 3⅛" (7.9cm x 7.9cm)

gold metallic paper: 3¾" x 3¾" (9.5cm x 9.5cm)

coordinating scrapbook paper
- green plaid print: 6" x 7" (15.2cm x 17.8cm) (2 total), 5½" x 4¼" (14cm x 10.8cm) (2 total), ½" x 4¼" (13mm x 10.8cm) (14 total), ½" x 3½" (13mm x 9cm) (3 total), 2" x 2" (5cm x 5cm)
- light brown natural print: 5¼" x 4" (13.3cm x 10.2cm)

book boards or sturdy mat board: 5⅝" x 4⅜" (14.3cm x 11cm) (2 total)

cotton linter squares (enough to cover mold)

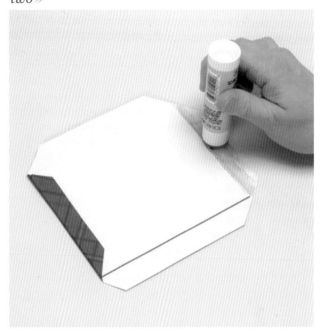

CREATE CASTING AND FIRST BOOK BOARD | Using the basic technique, create one trees paper casting. Substitute the leaf green cardstock for the copy paper for sizing and color. Take one book board and cover one side with a glue stick, then adhere it to the center of one of the 6" x 7" (15.2cm x 17.8cm) plaid papers. Turn it over and brayer the paper down, then turn it back over with the board side up. Using the other book board as a guide, pencil a diagonal line onto the paper at all four corners of the board.

GLUE AND WRAP AROUND THE SHORT TABS | Using scissors, cut along the pencil lines, removing paper in the corners. Beginning with one side, apply glue stick to the paper, up to and including the edge of the board. Using the table for leverage, roll the board up partway to adhere the paper to the board. Smooth down the paper the rest of the way. Repeat for the tab directly across from the glued tab.

GLUE THE REMAINING TWO SIDES | Using a bone folder or a thumbnail, crease the paper at the corners and then repeat gluing with the other two sides. Tap all sides firmly on the table to flatten, or smooth with a bone folder. Repeat gluing procedure for the other book board. Set aside.

ACCORDIAN FOLD CREAM CARDSTOCK | Take the larger piece of cream cardstock, and lay it on a cutting mat. Measure and score a line that is 2" (5.1cm) from one short end. Then score fourteen lines that are spaced ½" (13mm) apart, leaving 2" (5.1cm) at the opposite end. Beginning at one end, fold along the first score line and then fold in the opposite direction for the next score line. Continue alternating the direction of folding until the last score line has been folded. Apply pressure to the folded piece to set the folds.

five »

ADHERE ONE END TO BOARD | Take the book boards and lay them out with the plaid paper side down. Apply glue stick to one 2" (5.1cm) section on the end of the accordion folded cream cardstock piece and adhere to one book board at a short end. Make sure to center the cream cardstock.

six »

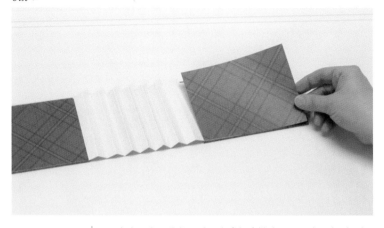

ADD LINERS | Attach the other 2" (5.1cm) end of the folded piece to the other book board in the same manner. Fold up the piece to ensure the boards align properly. Take the two green plaid pieces that are 5$\frac{1}{2}$" x 4$\frac{1}{4}$" (14cm x 10.8cm) and, using a glue stick, adhere one to the inside of each book board. Brayer down the paper.

seven »

ADD PAPER AND TREES TO COVER | Turn the album over so that you are looking at the front cover. Use a glue stick to adhere the light brown paper to the center of the album front. Punch four pine trees out of the small square piece of plaid paper. Using a glue stick, attach one pine tree on each corner of the light brown paper diagonally with the top of the trees pointing toward the outside.

eight »

LAYER GOLD AND GREEN SQUARES | Layer the square of green plaid paper onto the square of gold paper, using a glue stick. Brayer it down. Lightly mark the halfway points on the two short sides of the light brown paper. These markings will serve as a guideline for diagonally applying the layered papers.

nine »

ADD SQUARE PAPERS | Apply glue stick to the gold and plaid square piece and adhere it to the brown paper on the album cover. Remember to line up the points of the square with the pencil marks. Wrap the two extending points over the edges of the board and adhere to the back. Brayer the square piece down and flatten the wrapped edges with a bone folder.

ten »

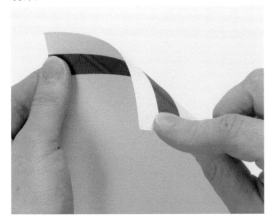

ADHERE STRIPS TO PAGES | Apply the ½" x 4¼" (13mm x 10.8cm) plaid strips to the remaining pieces of cream cardstock, as shown, using a glue stick. Apply one strip to the right side of one piece, " (13mm) from the outside. Flip the cardstock over and apply a second strip opposite and directly behind the first one. Repeat with the other six cream cardstock pieces, gluing strips to each.

eleven »

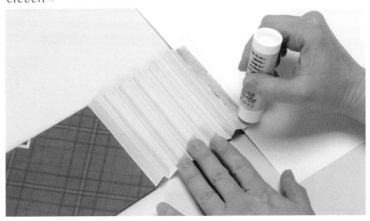

BEGIN GLUING IN PAGES | Open the album with the front cover to the left and the outsides of the book boards facing down. Starting from the back of the book and working forward, lay a piece of scrap paper under the first accordian fold, fold the first section down and apply glue stick.

twelve »

ADD PAGES | Insert one cream cardstock piece over the glue. Continue using the scrap paper to glue the right side of each fold and inserting the rest of the pages until the front of the album is reached.

thirteen »

COLOR SQUARE EDGES AND CASTING | Take the square of the sturdy textured white paper and dip it into the deep green ink pad on all four edges. Set aside to dry. Tear the flat end off of a cosmetic sponge and dip it into the deep green ink pad. Lightly dab on the color to the raised edges of the trees paper casting. Set aside to dry.

fourteen »

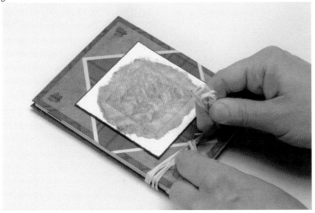

ADD CASTING AND RAFFIA TO FINISH | Use craft glue to apply the textured square paper to the center of the green plaid square as shown. Weight it down with a heavy book until the glue is dry. When dry, adhere the paper casting piece with craft glue to the center of the textured square. Weight it down with a book until the glue is dry. Tie several strands of raffia together in a bow along the left side of the album (this can be slid on and off of the album for use).

7 Paper weaving is yet another easy technique that looks much more difficult than it really is. The only rule you need to follow for this technique is to choose lightweight paper for the weaving and, if possible, to choose papers that coordinate together well. The pattern or picture on the paper is really not too important because, as you weave, the printed design usually becomes lost. The scrapbooking industry has really provided us with a large selection of coordinating papers, and even stickers and embellishments to match. Three projects are featured in this section, which include straight and wavy weaving techniques. This is an easy and great way to achieve a textured look.

Paper Weaving

YELLOW & BLUE CARD

ENVELOPE PORTFOLIO

FUNKY BOX

WEAVING
BASICS

Materials

For this technique, paper and scissors are all you really need, but I like to include a few other items, such as a base for weaving and glue to hold together all of my hard work. Most of the time, you will probably want to cut your own strips, but if not, you can purchase them in precut strips at your local craft supply store. Metallic or textured handmade papers add a lot of interest. Just make certain what you choose isn't too heavy, or your woven project could get a little unruly.

BASE CARDSTOCK

Choose a piece of cardstock that is larger than the desired finished size of the woven piece. This cardstock will provide a sturdy base for the finished product since the papers that you will be weaving with are thin and lightweight. You may wish to choose a cardstock that coordinates with the finished project in case little bits of the base cardstock show through between woven strips.

TWO COORDINATING PAPERS FOR WEAVING

Choose two coordinating papers for completing a paper weaving piece. You will be more successful if these papers are light-bodied and forgiving of creases. Suggested papers for weaving are Japanese washi paper, scrapbook paper, gift wrap paper and handmade paper.

GLUE STICK

I prefer using a glue stick when weaving paper, because it works well on thin papers. You will use it to secure all your woven paper strips throughout the project.

SCISSORS AND A PAPER CUTTER

Scissors and/or a paper cutter are necessary for cutting strips of paper and to neatly and accurately cut a finished woven piece down to the project size.

Techniques

Weaving paper is really just as easy as can be; all that's required is alternating back and forth between lifting and gluing every other strip. You'll be excited to see the results appear so quickly.

one »

LAY OUT A ROW OF STRIPS | Use a piece of cardstock larger than the desired finished size of the woven piece. Apply a line of glue stick across the top and then lay a row of light-bodied, ½" (13mm) wide strips of paper across the cardstock base as shown.

two »

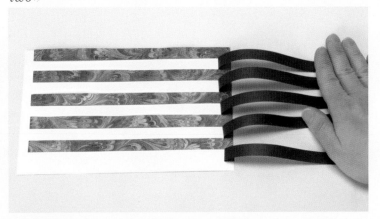

FOLD BACK ALTERNATE STRIPS | Gently fold back every other strip to prepare for weaving.

three »

LAY FIRST STRIP ACROSS THE ROW | Apply a line of glue stick across the strips that remain down and the base cardstock, just under the fold. Position a ½" (13mm) wide strip of paper across the existing strips as shown. Make sure the strip forms a right angle with the other strips.

four »

CONTINUE ALTERNATING ROWS | Apply a bit of glue stick underneath each strip as it is brought back down. Gently fold up the alternate strips and lightly crease those back to make room for the next strip. Continue this technique until the weave is complete. Always secure each piece with a glue stick as you go, and remember to keep all strips tightly nested together and even.

yellow & blue CARD

For this project I have chosen two coordinating scrapbook papers for the weaving technique and some layering possibilities. I have also added eyelets and thick gold thread to further enhance this card.

materials

- goldenrod cardstock (2 sheets)
- coordinating scrapbook paper
    navy print
    cream print
- navy ⅛" (3mm) eyelets (9)
- 2½ yards (2m) thick gold thread
- double-stick tape
- masking tape

- glue stick
- paper cutter
- scissors
- square scalloped punch
- Japanese screw hole punch
- protective surface for hammering
- eyelet setting tool
- hammer

PAPER PREPARATION ≫

Trim the following papers to the given sizes:

goldenrod cardstock: 11" x 5½" (28cm x 14cm), folded to 5½" x 5½" (14cm x 14cm), 5½" x 5½" (14cm x 14cm), 4¾" x 4¾" (12.1cm x 12.1cm), 2¼" x 2¼" (5.7cm x 5.7cm)

coordinating scrapbook paper:
- navy print: 5¼" x 5¼" (13.3cm x 13.3cm), 2½" x 2½" (6.4cm x 6.4cm) (2 total), ½" x 6" (13mm x 15.2cm) (11 total)
- cream print: ½" x 6" (13mm x 15.2cm) (11 total)

WEAVE NAVY AND CREAM STRIPS | Using the 5½" x 5½" (14cm x 14cm) goldenrod cardstock as a base, straight weave the navy print and cream print strips, and then use a paper cutter to trim the woven piece to 4½" x 4½" (11.4cm x 11.4cm). Layer this onto the 4¾" x 4¾" (12.1cm x 12.1cm) goldenrod cardstock piece, using double-stick tape.

ADD SCALLOPED SQUARE | Take one piece of 2½" x 2½" (6.4cm x 6.4cm) navy print paper and layer it with the 2¼" x 2¼" (.7cm x 5.7cm) golden-rod cardstock square. Using the square scalloped paper punch, punch a square out of the other 2½" x 2½" (6.4cm x 6.4cm) navy piece of paper and layer that on top of the goldenrod. Center this piece at a diagonal onto the woven piece and attach it using double-stick tape. Use the Japanese screw hole punch to make a hole in the center of the diagonal piece. Also, make a hole in each of the four corners of the scalloped punched piece and the four corners of the woven piece.

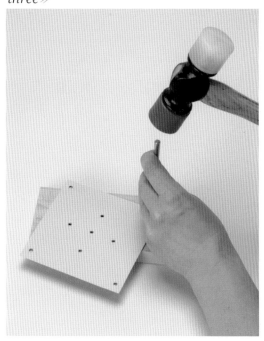

three

INSERT AND SET EYELETS | Insert an eyelet into each of the holes and set them with a hammer from the back, using an eyelet setting tool and a protective surface (see page 14).

Tip! **The projects for weaving in this book all use decorative paper or cardstock, but don't limit yourself. While thin papers are more forgiving to work with, try your luck with vellum sometime. The layering possibilities can be quite interesting. Another option is to use more than two colors, resulting in almost a plaid-type of look.**

four »

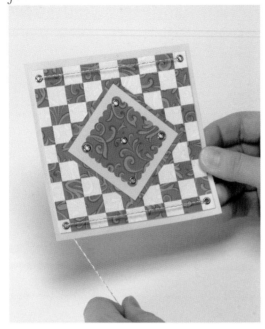

THREAD GOLD CORD | Wrap a piece of masking tape tightly around the end of the gold thread. Beginning from the back of the card, pull the gold thread through one of the corners on the outside of the card and secure with tape on the back. Come down through an adjacent hole, continuing in a clockwise fashion around the card.

five »

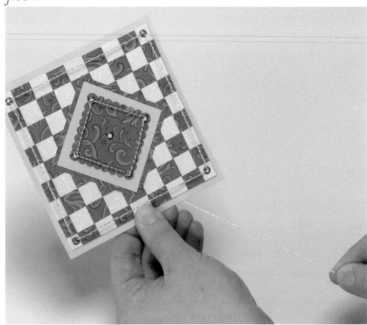

REPEAT THREADING ON SCALLOPED SQUARE | Come back through the starter hole and continue in the opposite direction. This completes a line of thread around all four sides. Repeat this same procedure on the inner scalloped square.

six »

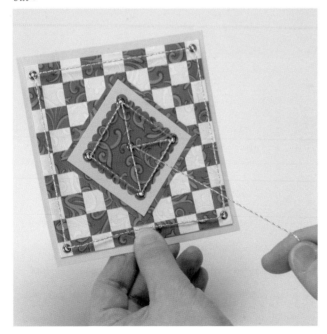

CREATE AN X IN THE CENTER | Come up through the center hole and then down through one of the scalloped corners. Come up through the center again and down through the next corner. Repeat on the other two corners, forming an x in the center of the scalloped square. Secure the end of the thread on the back with tape.

seven »

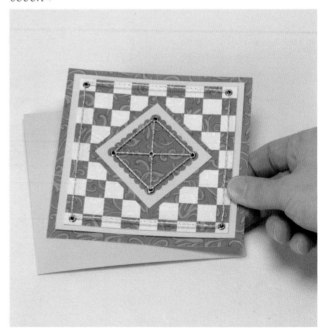

LAYER WOVEN PIECE ONTO CARD | Layer the woven piece onto the 5¼" x 5¼" (13.3cm x 13.3cm) navy print piece. Layer the finished piece onto the goldenrod fold-over card.

variation

ALTERNATE PAPER COMBINATIONS

CREATING CONTRAST

By combining a solid gold metallic paper with an elaborate patterned paper, I was truly able to show off the elegance of this lovely print. The simple layers finish the card for an end result that is subtle but sophisticated.

MAKE IT MONOCHROMATIC

The primary weave in this card uses three papers that are close in value. While the result is subtle, it provides a great backdrop for the dramatic dimensional flower, which really pops out.

envelope PORTFOLIO

This clever portfolio serves as a great way to store coupons, travel receipts, postage stamps and labels, or those special pictures. This project is bound using a system of plastic discs. You could easily substitute another type of binding system. Check out your local office supply or rubber stamp store for other binding ideas.

materials

- leaf green cardstock (2 sheets)
- cream cardstock
- gold metallic paper
- coordinating scrapbook paper
  light value
  dark value (2 sheets)
- cream envelopes
  4⅜" x 5¾" (11cm x 14.6cm) (5)
- gold glass micro beads
- double-stick tape
- glue stick

- masking tape
- clear-drying craft glue
- paper cutter
- Rollabind Personal Hand Punch
  Paper Guide
- Rollabind Personal Hand Punch
- Rollabind Binding Discs
  Matte Gold, Small (6)
- 1¼" (3.2cm) flower paper punch
- 1" (2.5cm) sun paper punch
- 1¼" (3.2cm) leaf paper punch

PAPER PREPARATION »

Trim the following papers to the given sizes:

leaf green cardstock: 5½" x 8½" (14cm x 216cm), 4⅜" x 5¾" (11cm x 14.6cm) (2 total), 4" x 3" (10.2cm x 7.6cm), 2¾" x 5⅛" (7cm x 13cm)

cream cardstock: 5½" x 2" (14cm x 5cm)

metallic gold paper: 4" x 1½" (10.2cm x 3.8cm), 3" x 5⅜" (7.6cm x 13.7cm)

coordinating scrapbook paper
- light value ½" x 5¾" (13mm x 14.6cm) (12 total)
- dark value 4¼" x 5½" (10.8cm x 14cm) (5 total), ½" x 5¾" (13mm x 14.6cm) (8 total), ½" x 5" (13mm x 12.7cm) (5 total)

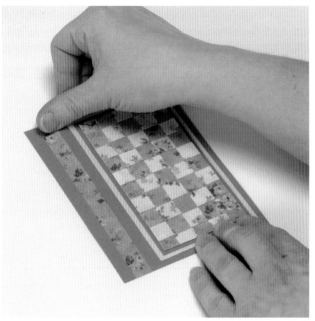

LAYER WEAVING AND STRIPS | Glue seven of the dark-value strips onto the green cardstock base and weave the light-value strips through as described in the basic techniques on page 91. Use a paper cutter to trim the woven piece to 2½" x 4⅞" (6.4cm x 12.4cm). Using double-stick tape, layer the woven piece onto the green 2¾" x 5⅛" (7cm x 13cm) piece of cardstock and then layer onto the gold paper that measures 3" x 5⅜" (7.6cm x 13.7cm). Layer this onto one of the 4⅜" x 5¾" (11cm x 14.6cm) green cover pieces, placing it on the right side, centered top to bottom. Using a glue stick, glue the remaining dark-value strip onto the left side, centered between the layered piece and the outside of the cover.

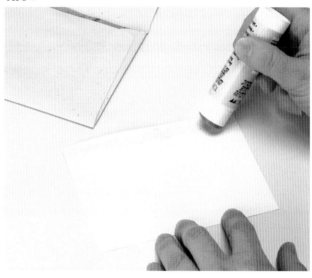

ADD ENVELOPE LINERS | Apply glue stick to one long edge of a 4¼" x 5½" (10.8cm x 14cm) dark-value paper piece and carefully slide it into an envelope, leaving the glued edge along the envelope fold. Repeat with the other four envelopes.

GLUE STRIPS ONTO ENVELOPE FLAPS | Use a glue stick to glue each ½" x 5" (13mm x 12.7cm) dark-value strip onto the envelope flaps about ¼" (6mm) from the edge.

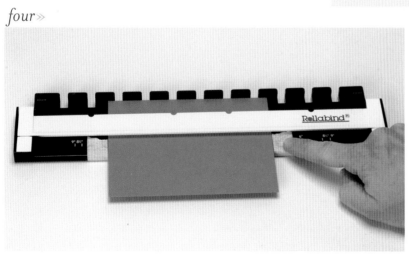

four

ALIGN COVER ON PUNCH GUIDE | Following the manufacturer's directions, center a green cover piece on the hand punch guide and mark the position of each edge with masking tape. This masking tape will help you keep the other items to be punched aligned in the same manner.

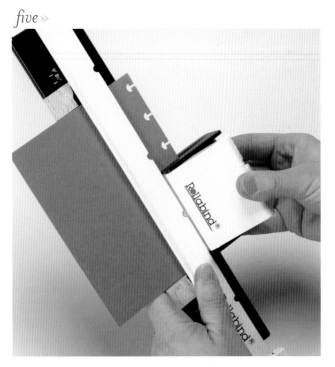

PUNCH COVER AND ENVELOPES | Use the Rollabind Hand Punch to punch holes into each cover and the five envelopes, using the masking tape marks as a guide. Remember not to punch the flap side of the envelopes.

INSERT BINDING DISCS | Arrange the outside covers and the envelopes with all holes aligned. Insert the gold discs. Don't be afraid of bending the paper a bit to get it around the disc.

ADD PUNCHED FLOWERS | Punch three flowers out of the cream cardstock, three suns out of gold metallic paper and six leaves out of leaf green cardstock. Use a glue stick to apply the sun in the center of a flower. Apply glue stick to the end of a leaf and attach it to the underside of the flower. Glue another leaf opposite the first leaf. Repeat with remaining three flowers. Glue finished flowers to the cover with a glue stick, in a random fashion as shown.

eight

SPOON BEADS ONTO FLOWER CENTERS | Apply clear-drying craft glue, in a circle, to the center of each flower about ¼" (6mm) in diameter. Spoon micro beads onto the glue, and gently knock excess beads off. Set aside to dry for at least one hour.

variations

PHOTO BOX

This store-bought storage box is given a unique lid treatment with the addition of this alternate weave piece. I added further interest with some layer pieces along the lid sides and some die-cut star pieces. The box is just the right size for photos or other cherished mementos. Match the paper to the color of the pre-existing cover paper.

ALBUM COVER

It's easy to spice up the cover of a simple photo album with a dramatic piece, like the one here. I just loved the look of a random pattern that was created when I mixed and matched the order of the three colors of paper strips. It was easy to complete in no time. I added decorative metal corners, a pretty bow and a special photo to complete the piece.

funky BOX

Papier-mâché boxes of all shapes and sizes are easily found in your local craft stores. They provide an inexpensive and great surface to work on. The possibilities are endless. This project is just one way to transform a papier-mâché box using paint, paper and a few embellishments to take the ordinary to extraordinary! I will also teach you how easy it is to create a wavy-style paper-weaving piece.

materials

- 5" x 5" x 2" (127mm x 127mm x 51mm) papier-mâché box
- lavender corrugated paper
- silver metallic paper
- decorative paper
    aqua
    lavender
- Royal Metallics Brilliant Silver textured paint (DecoArt)
- Americana Deep Periwinkle acrylic paint (DecoArt)
- Texturizing Medium (DecoArt)
- thick silver thread
- 20-gauge silver wire
- glass pebble
- silver leaf charm (2)
- glue stick

- clear-drying craft glue
- metal, glass and plastic glue
- scissors
- brayer
- 1-inch (2.5cm) flat paintbrush
- rubber bands
- palette paper
- toothpicks
- wire straighteners
- round-nose pliers
- wire cutters

PAPER PREPARATION »

Trim the following papers to the given sizes:

lavender corrugated paper: 4½" x 4½" (11.4cm x 11.4cm), 1" x 11" (2.5cm x 28cm) (4), ½" x 11" (13mm x 28cm) (2), ⅛" (3mm) wide (several assorted lengths), Cut all corrugated pieces perpendicular to the grooves

silver metallic paper: 5" x 5" (12.7cm x 12.7cm)

decorative paper
- aqua 5" x 6" (12.7cm x 15.2cm)
- lavender 5" x 6" (12.7cm x 5.2cm)

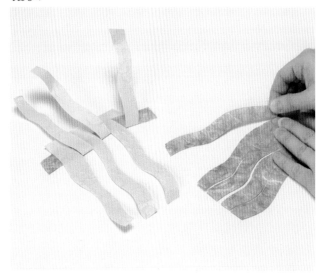

CUT WAVY LINES | Use scissors to cut a slightly wavy line along one long side of the aqua piece of paper, remaining as close to the outer edge as possible. Begin again at the bottom, and in a random wavy fashion, cut a strip that is approximately ½" (13mm) to ¾" (19mm) wide. Do not cut this strip all the way off, but leave it connected about ¼" (6mm) from the top. Continue cutting waving lines of the same width. When you reach the other side of the piece, cut off the last section. Repeat this process with the lavender piece of paper.

two

WEAVE STRIPS TOGETHER | Lay the aqua piece with the cut strips in a vertical position. Place the lavender piece so that the lines are in a horizontal position, and tear off the first strip. Fold every other strip of the aqua back and place a dot of glue near the folds on each strip that is down. Lay down the first lavender strip and fold the aqua strips back down. Fold up the next alternate strips and tear off the next lavender strip. Glue it to the aqua piece, using a glue stick. Repeat with all the remaining strips, keeping the wavy pattern aligned and nested tightly together. Brayer this finished piece down.

TRIM WOVEN PIECE | Following the curvy sides, cut off the excess paper. Repeat this procedure on all four sides, leaving a finished piece with curvy lines on all sides. If the finished size is too big for the box, remove a row or two to make it an appropriate size.

PAINT BOX AND LID INTERIORS | Paint the papier-mâché box. Start by painting the inside of the box as well as the inside and outside of the lid with the textured silver paint. Two coats may be needed. Set aside to dry.

five»

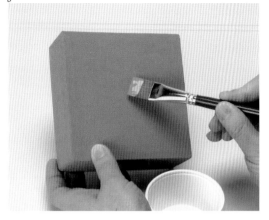

MIX PAINT | Mix the Deep Periwinkle paint with some of the Texturizing Medium, following the manufacturer's directions. Apply two coats to the outside of the box, allowing each coat to dry. Set aside to fully dry.

six»

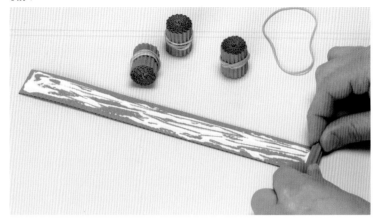

ROLL STRIPS FOR THE BOX LEGS | Gather the four 1" x 11" (2.5cm x 28cm) lavender corrugated pieces of paper. Run a line of clear-drying craft glue along the back of one piece and tightly roll it up. Be sure the piece sits flat. Secure it with a rubber band while the glue dries. Repeat with the remaining three pieces.

seven»

ADHERE STRIPS TO THE LID | Apply craft glue to the back of the square piece of lavender corrugated paper and adhere it to the lid of the box. Let dry, checking periodically for warping. Take the two corrugated ½" x 11" (13mm x 28cm) strips and, on the back, apply craft glue in a line down the center. Starting in the center of one of the box lid sides, attach the strip to the top edge. Apply glue to the second piece and butt it up to the first piece. Glue around until the two strips meet. Trim off the excess paper and wipe away any glue from the box and your scissors.

eight»

ADHERE SILVER THREAD TO THE LID | Place some craft glue on a piece of palette paper. Using a toothpick and working on one side at a time, dab some glue along the edge of the corrugated piece. Adhere the silver thread and smooth down. Where the two ends meet, trim off the excess silver thread with scissors. Any excess craft glue will dry clear. Repeat along all edges of the corrugated paper.

nine»

MOUNT LAYERS ONTO LID | Take the 5" x 5" (12.7cm x 12.7cm) piece of silver paper and, tearing toward you, tear away about ½" (13mm) of paper on all sides. Customize it to a size that will accommodate the corrugated piece on top of the lid and still show under the woven piece. Adhere the silver piece to the corrugated piece on top of the lid with a glue stick. Apply glue stick to the back of the woven piece and adhere on a diagonal to the silver piece.

ten »

ADD LEGS TO BOX | After the legs are completely dry, apply a generous puddle of craft glue to one end of each leg and attach them to the bottom of the box in the four corners. Set aside and allow ample time to dry.

eleven »

STRAIGHTEN WIRE | Work directly off the spool of wire and straighten a length of wire about 6" (15.2cm) long. Make one loop on the end of the wire with the round-nose pliers.

twelve »

CREATE WIRE SPIRALS | Grasp the wire loop in one hand and, with the remaining wire in the other hand, turn the wire to form a spiral. Trim the wire, leaving a tail that is approximately 1" (25mm) long. Repeat two more times to form a total of three spirals.

thirteen »

ADD GLASS PEBBLE AND LEAF CHARMS | Using a metal, glass and plastic glue, position wire spirals in a cluster, near the bottom corner of the woven piece. Apply a bit of glue to the glass pebble and then place the pebble over the ends of the wire. Apply a bit of glue to the silver leaf charms and position them under the pebble. Set aside to dry.

fourteen »

CREATE PAPER SPIRALS | Gather the strips of ⅛" (3mm) lavender corrugated paper and roll each tightly into a roll. Release and repeat for a total of about eleven pieces. Lay the corrugated spirals over the surface of the lid and arrange however looks best. Use a toothpick to apply craft glue to the edge of each piece and adhere them to the lid.

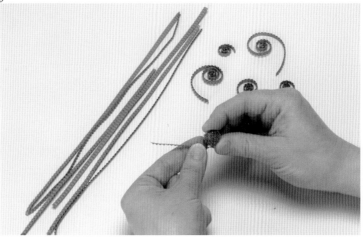

In this chapter you will learn how to create intricate, braidlike designs using lightweight paper. As with the technique of paper weaving, this method of folding paper does not require any discernable pattern on the paper you choose to use. Solids, metallics and Japanese washi paper all work equally well to create this cleverly crafted look. These designs are truly easy to create using a couple of different methods. The first two projects use a paper pattern and scissors, while the third project uses a metal template and a pointed craft knife. Whatever the method, you will be totally surprised at how easy it is to achieve this complex look!

Illusion Braid

BOOKMARK

BRAIDED SPINE CARD

BRAIDED MEDALLION CARD

BRAIDING
B A S I C S

Materials

The ability to make straight, smooth cuts is perhaps the key to success in this chapter. Therefore, lightweight papers and sharp cutting tools are the primary ingredients. With those and a pattern, you're ready to go!

COPY OF PATTERN

Use the pattern provided on this page to create a basic illusion braid. Either make a copy of it on a black-and-white copier, or trace the pattern using tracing paper. Once you learn this basic technique, you can experiment with different sizes of the pattern.

DECORATIVE PAPER

For this technique, lightweight paper such as washi, gift wrap and scrapbooking paper work best. Sometimes the color on the back of a piece of paper coordinates with the front, and you don't need two pieces. You can glue two lightweight papers together using a glue stick to create your own custom double-sided paper. Experiment with combinations you like together.

For learning the basic braiding technique used on the following pages, you will need a piece of 2" × 7½" (5cm × 19cm) paper. After you have mastered the basics, any size can be used.

GLUE STICK

Glue stick is used to mount two pieces of paper together, if a double-sided look is desired.

SCISSORS

Sharp scissors are a must. Dull scissors create a ragged edge, which makes pulling up layers to fold more difficult.

POINTED CRAFT KNIFE

A craft knife is needed to cut a template that isn't folded.

SELF-HEALING CUTTING MAT

You need a self-healing cutting mat when you cut through a pattern that isn't folded.

RULER OR STRAIGHT-EDGE

A ruler or straight-edge provides nice, smooth cuts for nonfolded patterns.

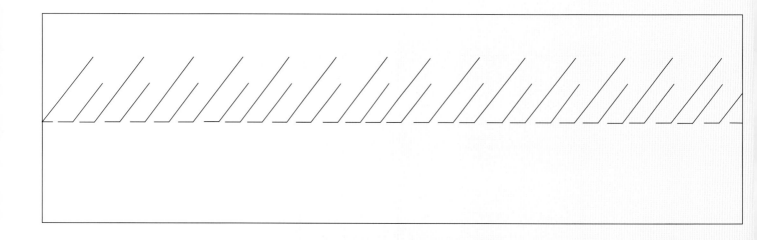

Techniques

Just cut and fold. That's really all there is to this beautiful method for creating interesting patterns and textures. The tip of a craft knife works great for picking up the pointed end when you're ready to start folding.

one »

FOLD PAPER AND PATTERN | Fold the project paper in half lengthwise and fold the pattern in half lengthwise with the pattern side out. Nest the folded paper inside of the folded pattern.

two »

CUT ALONG LINES WITH SCISSORS | Using scissors, cut along all indicated lines. Try to be precise with your cuts. The first line, at the top of the pattern, denotes that you will cut the first section completely off. Continue cutting along all indicated lines until you reach the bottom.

three »

FOLD UP FIRST V | Unfold both pieces and discard the pattern. Lay the cut paper flat on the table. Starting at the top, fold the second V up and crease as shown.

four »

ALTERNATE FOLDS | Repeat with every other V, folding up and creasing until you reach the end.

five »

TUCK IN POINTS | Lift up the first V that is pointing down, and tuck it under the V that is pointing up. Continue this process all the way down the piece of paper.

six »

TRIM EXCESS WITH A CRAFT KNIFE | Lay the finished cut and folded piece of paper onto the cutting mat. Using a craft knife and a ruler, cut away the paper on either side of the last V at the bottom as shown.

Tip! **Sometimes, when two papers are backed together, they will separate when folded. Simply flip the piece over and apply glue stick, using a tapping motion rather than a rubbing motion, and adhere any areas that have come apart.**

BOOKMARK

The simple illusion braid technique is quick to layer onto coordinating papers to create a one-of-a-kind bookmark. Add a tassel or some decorative fibers to complete the elegant look. This makes a great card enclosure for family and friends!

one »

COMPLETE ONE BRAID | Use a glue stick to adhere the back of the red print decorative paper to the back of the gold metallic paper. Set this double-sided piece aside to dry thoroughly, or it will be difficult to cut. When dry, trim this paper to the pattern size of 2" x 7½" (5cm x 19cm). Follow the instructions on page 107–108 to complete the illusion braid. Dab glue stick onto the back of the braid, center the piece on the black cardstock, and brayer it down.

materials

- black cardstock
- red corrugated paper
- gold metallic paper
- red print decorative paper
- black tassel
- glue stick
- copy of pattern on page 106
- scissors
- pointed craft knife
- cutting mat
- ⅛" (3mm) hole punch
- ruler or straight edge
- brayer

two »

ADD TASSEL | Apply glue stick to the back of the black cardstock and center it on the red corrugated paper. Use the ⅛" (3mm) hole punch to punch one hole at the top of the bookmark near the top of the V. Insert the loop of the tassel through the front of the bookmark to the back. Pull the tassel through the loop and pull it snug.

PAPER PREPARATION »

Trim the following papers to the given sizes:
black cardstock: 2¼" x 7¼" (5.7cm x 18.4cm)
red corrugated paper: 2½" x 7¾" (6.4cm x 19.7cm)
gold metallic paper: 3" x 8" (7.6cm x 20.3cm)
red print decorative paper: 3" x 8" (7.6cm x 20.3cm)

braided spine CARD

The same illusion braid pattern can be used to create a unique and special spine for a rubber-stamped and embossed card. What a wonderful way to add impact to all your card creations!

materials

- black cardstock
- gold metallic paper
- decorative paper
  (purple/gold/black print)
- black suede paper
- gold pigment ink pad
- gold embossing powder with glitter
- gold eyelets (4)
- butterfly metal charm
- glue stick
- ⅛" (3mm) thick foam tape
- copy of pattern on page 106
- scissors

- pointed craft knife
- cutting mat
- straight-edge
- brayer
- paint brush
- heat gun
- ⅛" (3mm) hole punch
- eyelet setting tool
- hammer
- protective surface for hammering
- decorative diamonds rubber stamp
  (Magenta)

PAPER PREPARATION »

Trim the following papers to the given sizes:

black cardstock: 10" x 7" (25.4cm x 17.8cm), folded to 5" x 7" (12.7cm x 17.8cm)

gold metallic paper: 3½" x 6" (9cm x 15.2cm), 3" x 8" (7.6cm x 20.3cm), ¼" x 7" (6mm x 17.8cm) (2)

decorative paper
- purple/gold/black print: 3" x 8" (7.6cm x 20.3cm)

black suede paper: 3½" x 5¾" (9cm x 14.6cm)

one »

CREATE BRAID AND TRIM | Using a glue stick, adhere the decorative paper to the 3" x 8" (7.6cm x 20.3cm) gold paper, back to back. Set aside to dry thoroughly. Trim to the pattern size of 2" x 7½" (5.1cm x 19.1cm). Follow the basic technique instructions (see page 107) to complete the illusion braid.

Match the top point of the braid to the top of the folded card. Look at the bottom of the fold and note which is the last V that will fit along the card. Trim the braid to that last full V as shown.

two »

LAYER BRAID TO SPINE | Dab a glue stick onto the gold side of the braid and lay the piece on the table with the glue side up. Line up the fold of the black card along the braid fold. Unfold the card and adhere it to the braid. Brayer it down.

It is important to glue the two layers together while they are both lying opened up and flat on the table.

three »

ADD GOLD STRIPS | Take the ¼" x 7" (6mm x 17.8cm) gold strips and, using the glue stick, adhere one strip to each side of the card along the edge of the illusion braid.

four »

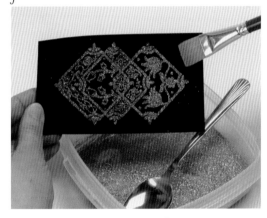

CREATE STAMPED IMAGE | Ink and stamp the rubber stamp image in the center of the black suede paper. Sprinkle on embossing powder, then use a paintbrush to brush away any loose powder that sticks to the suede paper. Heat with a heat gun to melt the embossing powder. Refer to the rubber-stamping chapter (beginning on page 16) for any questions regarding the use of a heat gun with embossing powders.

five »

LAYER CARD AND ADD CHARM | Using glue stick, layer the black suede paper onto the gold metallic paper that is 3½" x 6" (9cm x 15.2cm). Turn over and brayer down. Layer this onto the black fold-over card. Center it between the gold strip and the outside of the card. Using the ⅛" (3mm) hole punch, punch a hole in each corner of the black suede paper. Insert four gold eyelets and set using the eyelet tool, hammer and protective surface. Finish by adhering a small piece of ⅛" (3mm) thick foam tape under each wing of the butterfly charm and attaching it to the center of the card.

braided medallion CARD

This project uses a metal template to make easy work of creating a medallion pattern. The medallion shape is just another variation of what we have been exploring throughout this chapter. Look for many variations of this type of metal template at your local craft stores.

materials

- light green cardstock
- white cardstock
- coordinating scrapbook paper
  - light value
  - medium value
  - dark value
- deep green ink pad
- drafting tape
- glue stick
- Incire cutting template (Escatsy Crafts)
- cutting mat
- pointed craft knife
- scissors
- brayer
- "with love" rubber stamp

PAPER PREPARATION »

Trim the following papers to the given sizes:

light green cardstock: 7" x 10" (17.8cm x 25.4cm), folded to 5" x 7" (12.7cm x 17.8cm)

white cardstock: 3" x 1" (7.6cm x 2.5cm)

coordinating scrapbook paper
- light value 4" x 6" (10.2cm x 15.2cm)
- medium value 4¼" x 6¼" (10.8cm x 16cm)
- dark value 3¼" x 1¼" (8.3cm x 3.2cm), 4½" x 6½" (11.4cm x 16.5cm), 4½" x 6¼" (11.4cm x 16cm)

one »

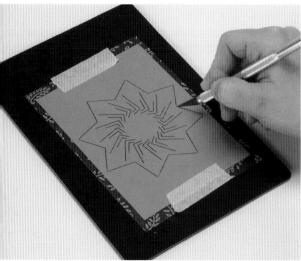

CUT DARK-VALUE PAPER | Place the cutting template on top of the dark-value paper that measures 4½" x 6¼" (11.4cm x 16cm). Secure with drafting tape. Place onto a cutting mat. Use a pointed craft knife to make cuts where indicated. When all cuts have been made, lift the paper up and check the underside to make sure everything is complete before removing your template.

Tip! **Keep a supply of fresh cutting blades on hand. Change blades when necessary to keep cuts nice and clean.**

two »

CUT OUT SHAPE | Remove the drafting tape and the template. Use scissors to completely cut out the perimeter of the star shape.

three »

BEGIN FOLDING V'S | Check the cut lines once again and make sure V's are entirely cut out and ready to fold. Use the pointed craft knife to complete cuts if necessary. Fold each V back, continuing around the shape.

four »

TUCK V'S UNDER | Now it is time to "lift and tuck" each section of the medallion. To do this, lift up the green paper and insert each white V underneath. Continue in this way all around the medallion.

five »

LAYER PAPERS AND BRAIDED PIECE | Using a glue stick, adhere the large dark-value paper to the light green fold-over card. Layer the medium-value paper and then the light-value paper to the card. Brayer down all layers. Using the deep green ink pad, stamp the "with love" message onto the white cardstock. Layer the stamped image onto the small piece of dark-value paper. On the top of the card, lay out the message and the braided piece. Dab glue onto the back of each piece and adhere.

In this chapter, we will close with two final techniques for paper. Both of these techniques can be easily adapted to many different projects and surfaces.

Tea bag folding (sometimes referred to as kaleidoscopic origami), was originally done with the packets tea bags come in. It is now done with small squares of decorative paper. The individual squares are folded in an origami-like fashion and then arranged together to make symmetrical designs. The project that will feature this technique is a flip-style portfolio, which can provide you with a great way to get organized by storing coupons, photos, travel receipts or sentimental mementos.

Paper quilting creates beautiful patterns similar to those found on hand-stitched quilts. Several different prints of paper are cut into various shapes and sizes and then adhered to a surface in an arrangement that mimics a quilt pattern. The project you will get to try a hand at, for this technique, is a lovely paper-quilted round box that could serve as a wonderful home accent for hidden treasures.

Both of these projects are perfect for gift-giving and, again, so simple that you'll want to reuse these techniques over and over! Because I've included only one project for each of these papercraft methods, we don't need to establish basic techniques, so let's just get started!

Tea Bag Folding & Paper Quilting

TEA BAG PORTFOLIO

PAPER QUILTED BOX

tea bag PORTFOLIO

Suggested papers for tea bag folding are Japanese washi paper, scrapbook paper, gift wrap paper or pre-printed paper squares made just for tea bag folding. A bone folder will aid you in folding and creasing your paper squares, and a two-way glue pen works great for quickly securing lightweight papers.

materials

- black cardstock
- gold metallic paper
- Japanese washi paper (red/gold print)
- Japanese washi paper (black/gold print)
- black envelopes 5¾" x 4⅜" (14.6cm x 11cm) (5 total)
- gold bow charm
- two-way glue pen
- double-stick tape
- glue stick
- adhesive-backed black hook and loop closure square
- clear-drying craft glue
- scissors
- bone folder
- 2¼" (5.7cm) scalloped heart punch
- paper cutter
- brayer

PAPER PREPARATION ≫

Trim the following papers to the given sizes:

black cardstock: 10" x 5¾" (25.4cm x 14.6cm) folded to 5¾" x 5" (14.6cm x 12.7cm), 3" x 3" (7.6cm x 7.6cm)

gold metallic paper: 5¾" x 3¾" (14.6cm x 9.5cm), 4¾" x 2¼" (12cm x 5.7cm), 3¼" x 3¼" (8.3cm x 8.3cm)

Japanese washi paper
- red/gold print: 5¾" x 3½" (14.6cm x 9cm), 5½" x 4¼" (14cm x 10.8cm) (5), 2" x 2" (5.1cm x 5.1cm) (4)
- black/gold print: 9" x 6" (23cm x 15.2cm), 4½" x 2" (11.4cm x 5cm), 2" x 2" (5cm x 5cm) (4)

one »

BEGIN FOLDING SQUARES |
Gather the four small red/gold print pieces and the
four small black/gold print pieces. Beginning with
one square, fold the square in half on the diagonal
and crease. Unfold and fold on the diagonal in the
opposite direction.

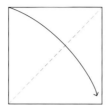 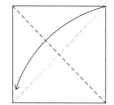

two »

 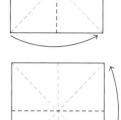

FOLD STRAIGHT | Unfold
and fold the piece in half. Unfold and
fold in half the other way.

three »

INVERT EACH SIDE | With the fold on
the bottom, invert one side. Push in and recrease,
leaving a 45° angle on one side. Invert the other
side to now form a triangle.

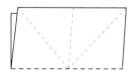

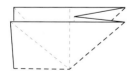

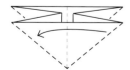

four »

TRIM CLEAN | Even up the cut side of the
paper if necessary with scissors.

five »

BRING OVER RIGHT SIDE | Lift up
the top triangle on the right side and fold it over to
the left side. Fold the point down to meet the bottom point.

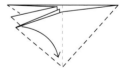

six »

BRING OVER SMALL TRIANGLE |
Then take the top small triangle you have just created and fold it over to the right side.

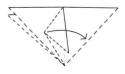

seven »

LIFT AND FOLD OVER TOP | Lift up the top triangle on the left side and flip it over to the right side. Fold the point at the top down to meet the bottom point.

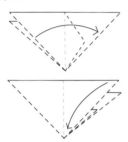

eight »

CREASE WITH BONE FOLDER | Fold the top small triangle you have just created over to the left side. Crease this final piece with the bone folder. Repeat these folds with the remaining seven squares (both red/gold and black/gold squares).

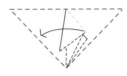

nine »

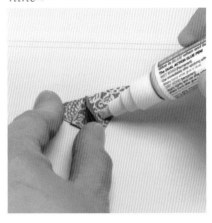

BEGIN ASSEMBLING PIECES | Begin with a red folded piece and place it point side down. Lift up the right-side small triangle and apply a dot of the two-way glue pen.

ten »

ADD A BLACK PIECE | Add a black folded piece against that fold as shown, overlapping the first piece.

eleven »

CONTINUE ALTERNATING COLORS | Lift up the right-side triangle of the black piece and apply a dot of the two-way glue pen and add another red piece. Repeat alternating colors until a complete circle is made.

twelve »

TUCK IN BLACK TO FINISH | To add the last piece, flip the small triangle of the last black folded piece back over to the left and apply a dot of the two-way glue pen. Bring the large red triangle that is in the back forward and adhere.

thirteen »

MOUNT TEA BAG PIECE | Using glue stick, mount the medallion piece to the square of black cardstock. Use double-stick tape to layer it onto the smallest piece of gold paper. Line each envelope with 5½" x 4¼" (14cm x 10.8cm) red/gold washi paper. Apply glue stick to one long side of each liner. Insert each into an envelope, with the glue at the fold. Punch five hearts from the large piece of black/gold paper. Adhere one heart to each envelope with glue stick.

fourteen »

BEGIN ADHERING ENVELOPES | Lay one envelope down, and apply glue stick over the flap. Lay another envelope on top of the flap against the fold of the bottom envelope.

fifteen »

CONTINUE ADDING ENVELOPES | Fold the bottom envelope up and apply glue to the next flap. Add a third envelope and again fold up. Glue the flap, then add the fourth envelope and fold up again. Glue the flap and add the final envelope.

It's important to fold up the envelopes as you go, to accommodate the bulk that builds up with each additional envelope.

sixteen »

ATTACH ENVELOPES INSIDE | Using a paper cutter, remove the last flap. Apply glue stick to the entire inside of the black fold-over card. While the fold-over card is lying flat on the table (glue side up), match the fold of the envelope portfolio packet to the fold of the black card. Adhere both layers together and brayer.

eighteen »

seventeen »

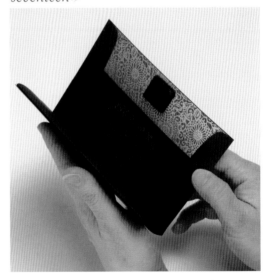

ADD HOOK AND LOOP CLOSURES | Trim away the excess cardstock from the envelope pack with the paper cutter. Fold the entire piece in half while the glue is still damp. With both squares of hook and loop closure together, remove the adhesive backing on one side, and apply to the card's interior. Remove the backing on the other side of the closure and close the card to adhere.

LAYER PORTFOLIO FRONT | Use a glue stick to apply the 5¾" x 3¾" (14.6cm x 9.5cm) gold layer to the portfolio front. Glue the remaining red/gold print piece to the gold paper. Layer on the last piece of gold paper and then the final piece of black print paper. Lastly, attach the layered tea bag piece to the center of the black print. Use clear-drying craft glue to apply the bow charm to the center of the medallion.

paper-quilted BOX

A papier-mâché box, paint, crackle medium and scrapbooking paper are combined in this project to create an elegant box with a quilted look. To create a paper quilt, you will need to choose a variety of coordinating paper. Many types of shape templates and sometimes special cutters to go along with them are available in your local craft stores.

materials

- round papier-mâché box
  7¾" x 3" (19.7cm x 7.6cm)

- five coordinating prints of scrapbook paper (labeled A through F, 1 sheet each)

- acrylic paint:
  Dazzling Metallics Glorious Gold (DecoArt)
  Americana Celery Green (DecoArt)

- Weathered Wood Crackling Medium (DecoArt)

- acrylic sealer/finisher, gloss

- metal heart charm

- glue stick

- clear-drying craft glue

- 1-inch (25mm) flat brush

- shape cutter

- shape templates
  circles
  squares
  rectangles
  diamonds
  hearts

- brayer

- scissors

one »

PAINT BOX GOLD | Apply two coats of Glorious Gold paint to the inside and outside of the entire box and allow to dry.

two »

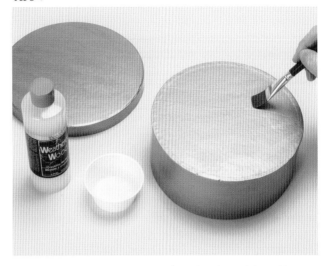

ADD CRACKLING MEDIUM | Apply one coat of the crackling medium to the outside of the box and the outside of the lid. Follow manufacturer's directions regarding drying time, which is usually about one hour.

three »

ADD CELERY GREEN | Apply one coat of the Celery Green to the outside of the box and the outside of the lid. Apply the paint in one direction only and try to load your brush with enough paint to coat the surface in one swipe. Crackles will begin to form within minutes. Allow to dry thoroughly.

four »

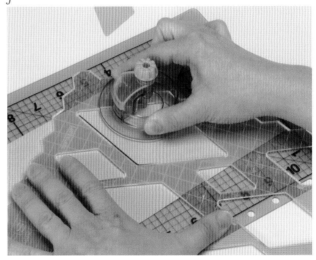

CUT SHAPES | Gather five pieces of scrapbook paper. Out of paper A, cut six diamonds that are 2¾" x 1½" (7cm x 3.8cm) using the shape cutter and the assorted templates according to the manufacturer's directions. Continue with the shape cutting system to cut out of paper B, six 1½" (3.8cm) hearts. Out of paper C, cut six 1½" (3.8cm) circles and six 2" (5cm) squares. Out of paper D, cut six 2" x 1" (5cm x 2.5cm) rectangles. Out of paper E, cut six 3¾" x 2" (9.5cm x 5cm) diamonds, and out of paper F, cut six 1½" (3.8cm) hearts and one 3" (7.6cm) circle.

Tip! **While a shape-cutting system makes the production of uniform shapes fast and easy, it is not too difficult to make your own templates out of matboard, or to use shapes on existing plastic templates. Trace either one with a pencil, then cut out the shapes with scissors or a craft knife.**

five »

GLUE LARGE DIAMONDS TO LID | Evenly space and apply the six diamonds from paper E onto the lid using a glue stick. The points will all meet in the center. Brayer down all pieces.

six »

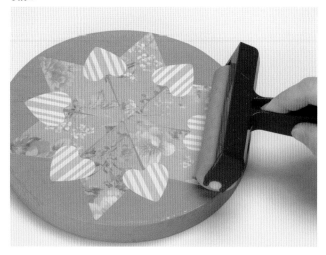

ADD FIRST SET OF HEARTS | Evenly space and apply the six hearts from paper F, using a glue stick. Glue each heart between but overlapping the diamonds, with the point about ¾" (19mm) from the outside edge of the lid.

seven »

ADD REMAINDER OF DIAMONDS | Evenly space and apply the six diamonds from paper A over the hearts, with a glue stick. Align the points meeting in the center, about ⅜" (10mm) from the points of the hearts.

eight »

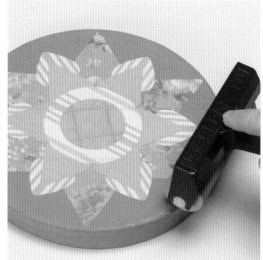

ADHERE CIRCLES | Center the paper F circle, using a glue stick. Then adhere the paper C circle in the center of the larger circle.

nine »

ADD LID TRIM | From paper E cut three strips that measure ¼" x 12" (6mm x 3cm). Apply glue stick to the strips and adhere them to the center of the rim of the lid. Butt the pieces together to complete the circumference of the lid, and trim off the excess if necessary.

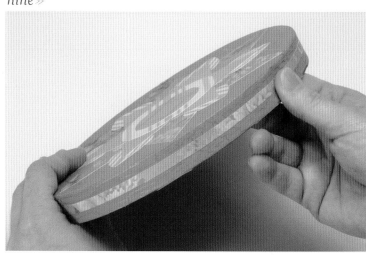

ten »

USE LID FOR PLACEMENT | Place the lid on the box to use the shapes on top as a template to space the remaining shapes evenly around the box sides (example: align squares with the points of the diamonds). With a glue stick, adhere the squares from paper C to the box.

eleven »

ADD RECTANGLES | Use a glue stick to apply the six rectangles from paper D. Center each one between the squares.

twelve »

ADD HEARTS | Use a glue stick to apply the six hearts from paper B in the center of each square. Allow everything to dry.

thirteen »

APPLY PROTECTIVE SEALER | Remove the lid and spray the inside of the box and the inside of the lid with the gloss acrylic sealer. Allow to dry. Then spray the outside of the lid and the box, and allow to dry.

fourteen »

ADD CHARM TO FINISH | Lastly, attach the large heart charm with craft glue and allow to dry.

RESOURCES

All the materials used for the projects in this book should be readily available at your local craft, rubber stamp or scrapbooking store. If you run into trouble, contact the manufacturers listed here for retailer information.

Paper »

DAISY D'S PAPER COMPANY
(888) 601-8955 phone
(801) 782-2162 fax
www.daisydspaper.com
•Scrapbooking supplies

EK SUCCESS, LTD.
www.eksuccess.com
•Scrapbooking supplies

GREG MARKIM, INC.
(800) 453-1485 phone
(414) 453-1495 fax
www.arnoldgrummer.com
•Arnold Grummer's paper casting and paper making supplies

K&COMPANY, LLC
(888) 244-2083 phone
(816) 389-4156 fax
www.kandcompany.com
•Scrapbooking supplies

MARCO'S PAPER
(888) 433-5239 phone
(888) 266-0496 fax
www.marcopaper.com
•Paper supplies

PAPER ADVENTURES
(800) 727-0699 phone
(800) 727-0268 fax
www.paperadventures.com
•Paper supplies

PAPERS BY CATHERINE
(713) 723-3334 phone
(713) 723-4749 fax
www.papersbycatherine.com
•Paper supplies and tassels

PROVO CRAFT
(800) 937-7686 phone
(801) 794-9006 fax
www.provocraft.com
•Scrapbooking and general craft supplies

Rubber Stamps »

INKADINKADO
(800) 888-4652 phone
(781) 938-5585 fax
www.inkadinkado.com
•Rubber stamps and accessories

MAGENTA RUBBER STAMPS
(450) 922-5253 phone
www.magentarubberstamps.com
•Rubber stamps and accessories

RIVER CITY RUBBER WORKS
(877) 735-2276 phone
(316) 529-8940 fax
www.rivercityrubberworks.com
•Rubber stamps and accessories

STAMPENDOUS
(800) 869-0474 phone
(800) 578-2329 fax
www.stampendous.com
•Rubber stamps and accessories

Inks & Adhesives »

AMY'S MAGIC
(724) 845-1748 phone
•Tacky embossing powder, tacky adhesives and gold leafing

BEACON ADHESIVES COMPANY, INC.
(800) 865-7238 phone
(914) 699-2783 fax
www.beacon1.com
•Adhesives

CLEARSNAP, INC.
(800) 448-4862 phone
(360) 293-6699 fax
www.clearsnap.com
•Inks and ink pads

GLUE DOTS INTERNATIONAL
(888) 688-7131 phone
(262) 814-8505 fax
www.gluedots.com
•Adhesive dots

STEWART SUPERIOR CORPORATION
(800) 558-2875 phone
(800) 427-1717 fax
www.stewartsuperior.com
•Memories inks and ink pads

TOMBOW
(800) 835-3232 phone
(678) 318-3347 fax
www.tombowusa.com
•Adhesives

TSUKINEKO, INC.
(800) 769-6633 phone
(425) 883-7418 fax
www.tsukineko.com
•Brilliance and Encore Ultimate Metallics inks and ink pads

Cutting, Punching & Stenciling Tools »

AMERICAN TRADITIONAL DESIGNS
(800) 448-6656 phone
(800) 448-6654 fax
www.americantraditional.com
•Overlay stencils, brass stencils

FISKARS BRANDS, INC.
(800) 500-4849 phone
(715) 848-3657 fax
www.fiskars.com
•Crafting and cutting supplies

HERITAGE HANDCRAFTS
(303) 683-0963 phone
(303) 683-0965 fax
www.heritage-handcrafts.com
•Brass stencils and supplies

MCGILL, INC.
(800) 982-9884 phone
(815) 568-6860 fax
www.mcgillinc.com
•Paper punches

UCHIDA OF AMERICA, CORP.
(800) 541-5877 phone
(800) 229-7017 fax
www.uchida.com
•Paper punches

Embellishments »

ACCENT FACTORY
A Boutique Trims Company
(888) 437-3888 phone
(248) 437-9463 fax
www.boutiquetrims.com
•Metal charms and embellishments

KREINIK MANUFACTURING CO., INC.
(800) 537-2166 phone
(410) 281-2519 fax
www.kreinik.com
•Threads, cording and braids

Paints & Other Mediums »

CRAF-T PRODUCTS, INC.
www.craf-tproducts.com
•Metallic Rub-Ons

DECOART
(800) 367-3047 phone
(606) 365-9739 fax
www.decoart.com
•Paints and other mediums

Other Products »

ECSTASY CRAFTS
(888) 288-7131 phone
(613) 968-4271 fax
www.ecstasycrafts.com
•Parchment craft supplies and Incire templates

LAKE CITY CRAFT COMPANY
(417) 725-8444 phone
(417) 725-8448 fax
www.quilling.com
•Quilling supplies

OLD TOWN CRAFTS
(877) 313-6745 phone
(912) 576-3663 fax
www.oldtowncrafts.com
•Rubber stamps, embossing powders and rhinestones

ROLLABIND, LLC
(800) 438-3542 phone
(954) 972-2930 fax
www.rollabind.com
•Binding systems

WALNUT HOLLOW
(800) 950-5101 phone
(608) 935-3029 fax
www.walnuthollow.com
•Wood products and Creative Hot Marks tool

INDEX

The best in creative crafting

IS FROM NORTH LIGHT BOOKS!

VINTAGE GREETING CARDS WITH MARYJO MCGRAW

Let MaryJo McGraw, renowned rubber stamp artist and card maker, show you how to create handmade cards that capture the look and feel of antiques and heirlooms. You'll create 23 gorgeous cards using easy-to-find heirloom papers, old family photos and ephemera.

ISBN 1-58180-413-X, paperback, 128 pages, #32583-K

THE ESSENTIAL GUIDE TO MAKING HANDMADE BOOKS

Gabrielle Fox teaches you how to create your own handmade books, one-of-a-kind art pieces that go beyond the standard definition of what a "book" can be. You'll find 11 projects inside. Each one builds upon the next, just as your skills increase. This beginner-friendly progression ensures that you're well prepared to experiment, play and design your own unique handmade books.

ISBN 1-58180-019-3, paperback, 128 pages, #31652-K

CREATIVE STAMPING WITH MIXED MEDIA TECHNIQUES

In this exciting book, Sherrill Kahn shows you how to create unique and stunning effects by combining sponging, glazing and masking techniques with stamped patterns in bold colors. Through 13 step-by-step projects and 20 dramatic paint and stamping recipes, you'll create amazing projects on a range of surfaces including a wooden tray, terra cotta flowerpot, journals, boxes and more.

ISBN 1-58180-347-8, paperback, 128 pages, #32315-K

CREATIVE CORRESPONDENCE

Michael and Judy Jacobs show you how to create spectacular decorative mail! You'll find 15 step-by-step projects, including letters and envelopes with photo inserts, stapled booklets and acetate address windows, plus clever self-mailers. With the basic techniques, embellishments and decorative techniques demonstrated inside, you'll achieve great-looking results from start to finish.

ISBN 1-58180-317-6, paperback, 96 pages, #32277-K

These books and other fine North Light titles are available from your local arts and crafts retailer, bookstore, online supplier or by calling (800) 448-0915.